BAGS OF
MICE

Z.C. CHRISTIE

BAGS OF
MICE

Z.C. CHRISTIE

8 Bags of Mice

Cover Design by Booklocker Express

Interior Design by Gwen Gades

INTRODUCTION, DEDICATION, PREFACE, ACKNOWLEDGMENT, FORWARD, BACKWARD, ONWARD AND UPWARD, ETC.

Did I leave out any of these "official" book declarations? The words or blurbs that are in the front of *every* book I pick up?

I didn't want those statements in the front of this book. I do realize people are used to seeing this sort of thing, but here are my feelings on the matter: You won't to come to know me by reading any declarations stuffed in the front of a book. You won't discover why I write as I do, unless *you* read what I've written... not what someone *else* thinks of what I've written.

If you read my scribblings and like what you've found, why not write and tell me your thoughts on them? I would love to hear from you, really.

So go forth, read... see what you discover and hopefully, I'll hear from you soon.

zcchristie@yahoo.com

CONTENTS

IN THE
BEGINNING...

I never planned on writing a book. I've scribbled stuff ever since I was small… filled notebooks, kept journals, and I am a prolific list maker. But write a book? About what?

I didn't have these massive, epic stories in my head like the big shots of literature. I wasn't full of spiritual insights or revelations that I felt compelled to share with mankind. I had no real expertise, degree, or special training in anything technical, inventive, or otherwise, unless you count managing Continual Crisis and Chaos in a Slightly Crazed Family.

All I had was an endless stream of notes, thoughts, anecdotes about my family, little stories of things I had experienced or had caught my interest, and a bunch of lists.

Nothing that was going to make a big splash in the literary world, or get me invited to appear on a late night talk show, where I would chatter away about the book, while trying to keep the world from seeing up my skirt by keeping my legs tightly crossed. (Have you ever noticed how those damned cameras seem to be aimed right at the guest's crotch? And nearly all of the female guests wear a skirt or a dress? And then they spend most of their air time tugging the hem down?) Not for me, no thanks.

People have asked if I write for Fame, Fortune, and Recognition… and I guess they're not bad things to have, some people seem to want that sort of thing. Fame, well, my language is a tad colorful at times, and any interview with me would inevitably have a series of *beeeeps*. Fortune is always handy in anyone's life, but it truly isn't everything. Recognition? If I look in a mirror every day and know who the heck I am, that's good enough for me. So no, I don't write to try and achieve those things.

I write because all those words, thoughts, memories, and junk whirling around in my brain have to be purged on occasion, or my head would explode. I don't *want* my head to explode, as it's the only one I have and I sort of need it. There is only one way for me to purge all that built up junk, and that is by writing it down.

So what you will read from me are my true thoughts, actual stories and memories, real reactions, desires, hopes, fears, phobias, bad habits, and everything else.

I have been told that some of these stories, especially those about Husband, are amusing (trust me, they weren't funny at the time). It's not all I write, though. So don't be surprised if in some tales you see me whine, get bitchy, make stupid ass decisions, become sad, or even heartbroken. I'm just like you and experience these sorts of feelings, so I write about them. It's how I survive emotionally, sometimes.

On Being Anonymous: My kids, after reading the stuff I wrote about them, reminded me that they had to live and work on this planet, and if I *had* to do this project, could I at least do it anonymously? To keep these silly people happy, I decided to borrow ancient family names (from long dead family members, they won't mind) to use in place of my own. But you'll get to know the real me through what I write, and that's what counts anyway, isn't it?

So, hello there…it's really great to meet you.

Z.C.

LIFE IN LOUISIANA

YOU'RE MOVING WHERE?

There were a goodly number of my Northern friends and relatives, who upon learning that we were relocating from the Midwest to the Deep South, called or emailed me to express varying degrees of concern.

They had seen the infamous Mardi Gras footage on television for many years, showing tourists and college students partying or vomiting in the streets, drunk as a skunk and tearing their clothes off. *This* is where I was moving with my *children?* On purpose? No one they knew moved to such a place on *purpose.*

Were we sure of what we were doing?

Did I know it was called the Deep South for a reason? Why didn't we just move back up North? There were probably swamps and pits of quicksand down there! What if the people weren't *civilized?*

Everyone reacted as though I planned on moving with the family to the wilds of Borneo, or someplace… sheesh, its only Louisiana, people, relax. I assured everyone that we had landed in an actual jet in an actual airport, interviewed without incident, had toured the town and seen people driving cars and wearing shoes. We had seen evidence of computers, cell phones, and everyone at dinner had used a knife, fork and spoon, the same as we did.

I didn't witness one soul getting drunk or taking off a single piece of clothing. Husband accepted the contract, we packed up the house, the kids, all the animals, said farewell to the Midwest and drove south to our new home in Looz-ee-anna or Weezy-anna, as the natives pronounced it, depending on their accent.

The local people were wonderful, you would never meet a stranger. Everyone said hello and smiled, or waved as they drove or walked by. People you met while waiting in line or riding on an elevator would strike up a conversation, discover that you were new to the area and invite you over for dinner. And mean it.

You quickly learn Southerners will say anything about another person, even if it's not terribly polite, as long as it has the phrase, "bless his/her heart" tacked onto it.

"You've gained at least 30 pounds, I swear you have, baby, bless your heart."

"I declare, darlin', that color makes you look downright jaundiced, doesn't it? Bless your heart."

"Miss Rose, is that fat man over there in that awful suit your husband? Bless his heart."

Everyone, regardless of age, calls one another by their first names, with a Mister or Miss on the front. A four year old child could greet a 90 year old woman by saying, "Hey there, Miss Adeline!" and that is perfectly acceptable in the South. It threw me into Gone With the Wind mode daily, until I became accustomed to it, and even though I moved away from there many years ago, I still greet folks that way.

Food and music are both major things in Cajun Country. I'm allergic to a lot of seafood, so I never indulged in the vast number of dishes Southerners could concoct from this stuff. My boys became addicted to boudin (*boo-dan*), gumbo, jambalaya, and learned how to eat crawdads properly...you bite the heads off and suck out the juices.

Zydeco music plays from the speakers in public parks on all the holidays, everyone dances a lot and you can buy alligator-meat-on-a-stick at the street fairs. You can carry alcohol in your car as long as it's in plain sight, and there are drive-through daiquiri bars all over town.

We lived in Louisiana for four years. It was an adventure sometimes, and for us transplanted Northerners, it took some getting used to on many levels: the heat... the bugs... the mold... the fire ants... the heat... the pronunciation of French surnames... the food... the heat.

Would you like it if I went into greater detail on a few of these topics, if you ever decide to move there yourself, or visit someday? Hey, you never know, some of this stuff could come in handy. We will start with the heat...

SOUTHERN HEAT

South Louisiana has the two distinct seasons, Hot and Not As Hot.

Summertime is a literal steam bath. I learned to buy nothing but cotton and linen clothing, and stopped wearing underpants except for the, oh, about six to eight weeks it was a little less humid down there. Absolutely no pun intended, but it was funny how that came out, wasn't it?

I am sure Louisiana natives wore underpants, only I was a transplanted Northerner who didn't see any sense in wearing sweaty undergarments that stuck to me, making my outer clothes all sweaty and wet in return. So off they came. The undergarments, not my *clothes*.

The humidity is so intense, you can walk outside and get wet, whether it is raining or not. My unofficial name for Louisiana was The Crotch Rot State.

MOLD

All that talk about damp panties leads us to the topic of mold. Mold is everywhere, nearly all the time. There is black mold and green mold and sometimes a lovely patterned combination of the two, all shiny and slippery.

Boy, is it slippery, and it creates big, slick, greeny-black areas where the endless damp and heat combine to make places where a person can easily slip and fall down, like I used to do all the time, until I learned to step around the damned stuff. The North has ice that you slip and fall on, but the Deep South has mold.

It's on the buildings, on the trees, it's on anything you leave outside longer than a day. Clothes left outside grow mold. Lawn cushions, baskets, sneakers, and paperbacks you forgot to bring inside because you were silly enough to try and read outdoors. If you sat out in all that humidity long enough, you'd probably grow mold, too.

GUNS AND WEAPONS

Guns n' weapons are a fact of life, for both sexes, down South. Most kids, by the age of eight, owned some sort of gun or knew how to shoot one. My very sweet, genteel neighbor lady was all thrilled when her husband bought her a new gun one Christmas. I tried to look impressed when she showed it to me, but all I could think of was, she wears flowery dresses or floaty skirts all the time, served me tea from an expensive antique silver tea set, and yet was gushy about a big ole *gun.*

She was less gushy a week later, because her husband had loaded the gun one night as they were sitting on the bed, was fiddling with it and somehow shot a hole clear through the mattress and box spring and into the floor.

Not only had he ab-suh-loot-lee *roont* her bed linen, she informed me, but she had wanted to be the one to shoot it fuhst, aftah awl, it was *her* gun.

Yeah, sure, I understand completely.

MOSQUITOES AND LIZARDS

Mosquitoes are available 24 hours a day, seven days a week, except for the week of Christmas. Kidding, they're gone by about November 30th and don't come back for a month or so. The lizards eat the mosquitoes, the moths, and lots of other icky insectoid critters, so if you are down South and see lizards on your window screens, in your car, or skittering around in your house, be very happy they are there and please do not squash them.

IF YOUR VEHICLE
BREAKS DOWN

If you are stranded on the road with a broken vehicle and lots of other cars or trucks pull up and guys hop out and offer to help you, don't panic. This is the South. Guys will scrunch under your car (even if it's raining) or lift the hood and tinker with the engine until your vehicle starts. And if it's not fixable, everyone down South has a truck or knows someone who owns a truck and they will haul your vehicle to a garage for you. Then invite you over for dinner.

ATTACK OF LA CUCARACHA

Which translated, means attack of the cockroach, but they don't really attack, they just sort of lay (or is it lie?) in wait. If you move down South, you need to face the fact that a lot of bugs live there, indoors and outdoors. We had bugs up North, but most types of bugs I was accustomed to seeing back home, had startlingly larger cousins down South.

Worms are bigger, moths are huge, and the roaches (called tree roaches in Louisiana) can *fly*. I have never researched to see if non-Southern roaches fly. I am sure they might, I just don't care to know, since I discovered Louisiana tree roaches can and do fly. All over.

Like at you, or into your hair. And why they are called tree roaches make no sense, since they are not just in trees, but everywhere.

In your closet, as you reach for that pair of shoes… under the kitchen sink, as you reach for the can of cleanser… in the bathroom, right at the bottom of the basket you just took that fluffy towel out of… big, long, antennae waving Everywhere Roaches.

They are so big, they don't even scuttle away at the sight of a human like the occasional Northern roaches I had seen. No, they do things like calmly walk out from under your bed as you are standing by it in your bare feet.

Perhaps you had just woken up, and were staring out the big picture window at the muddy water (we lived on the bayou, which is Louisiana waterfront, but it's just non-moving muddy water) wondering if that was a snake you just saw slither across the surface of the water, when your peripheral vision detects a slight movement…

You look down to see what it could be…and then *hurl* your body to safety in the middle of the bed and scream as loudly as you can for Husband to "*COME AND KILL THIS*

GODDAMNED ROACH!"

Husband is a big, tall guy, but he happens to hate roaches, especially *big* roaches. Too bad.

You're more of a match for it, honey, my heart rate is still over 200, *you* do battle with it. If I try to kill it in my present state, it will probably just laugh and then call all its friends to come on over and party.

I learned to keep a supply of clear plastic drinking glasses handy, that the kids were forbidden to drink from. If Husband was at work, you could recruit one of the teenagers to pop a glass over a roach if you found one. Trap it and then call Husband on the phone to say, "This one is *three inches, WHEN* can you get over here and get it out of the house?"

If he couldn't make it home right away, you then put something heavy on top of the glass, so the roach couldn't perhaps knock it over and escape, probably on a path right for you. Two big books work well for this. You carefully keep a secure area around the glass until Husband gets home, looks at the Roach Under Glass and announces for the hundredth time he *hates* big bugs and why does *he* have to be the one to take it outside?

If you ever move down South with a bug loathing Husband who whines about these things, keep a supply of those cardboard rectangles that come in new shirts and stuff. They're good for sliding under the glass and trapping the roach in there, so you can then carry it outdoors without ever having to touch it. You then just *fling* the entire thing over the deck railing to the lawn below and run back into the house. The lawn guy will eventually bring the glass back and set it on the deck.

In the absence of a Husband, teenaged boy-type-kid or a kindly male neighbor being available to entrap a roach under glass, the solution is simple. You simply go shopping until someone that isn't you, *does* get home and can then be forced to search/shake/kick everything in the house to try to find the roach you saw sitting there earlier, as plain as day.

SNAKES

Louisiana has snakes, at least five poisonous species, last I heard. I didn't bother to verify this information online when informed of this, figuring it was safer to simply avoid any and all snakes while I lived there. Ha.

You can try to avoid them, but if you live near the water, they just come up on their own to check you out. We lived in a big house built on top of dozens of four foot cement pillars, on a property that bordered on the bayou. The house was constructed this high because the bayou flooded its banks every time it rained, and our house was the only one on the block that didn't have an adequate retaining wall.

Remnants of an old wall were visible along the waterfront, but rain meant that the water crept right up to the back deck *over* the collapsed, sunk-in-the-mud wall. Growing down by the remnants of the flood wall were tall, messy bunches of leafy plant type things, a perfect hang-out spot for snakes such as water moccasins... cottonmouths, some folks call them. They are venomous, aggressive and smelly. These snakes smell *awful,* they are mean, territorial as all get out, and they will come right after you if they think you're on their turf.

Our house had an upstairs balcony off one of the bedrooms. I was sweeping it clean one afternoon and happened to glance over the railing at a big pile of dirt on the lawn below. Landscaping was going on and dirt was all over, uprooted plants, etc.

One of our younger cats was batting a paw at a section of black hose lying on top of the dirt pile, and I thought, who in the heck cut up the hose? Husband is not going to be happy over that...and then the hose moved and one end lifted and *hissed* at the cat.

Snake. Black snake. *Big,* long black snake, right below me, hissing at the cat. I screamed, of course, and then threw the broom at it like a spear (wondering as I did, if snakes could climb balconies) and judging my distance to the door, in case it decided to leap at me. The snake didn't kill the stupid cat that was still batting at it, but instead, slithered off the pile of dirt and disappeared directly under my deck.

My deck. The part that was right outside my back door, where I came in and out of a dozen times a day, my kids, too. Right there under *my deck,* which was wooden and had spaces in between the boards where an evil snake could possibly poke its head through and bite someone I loved.

I called Husband, who naturally said I was overreacting, and that the snake was probably gone by now. I overreacted a lot more and said I *knew* the snake wasn't gone. So I went out the front door (which was on level ground, no deck underneath) to run over to where the neighbor's lawn man was working and told him what I had seen.

He went and got a gun out of his pickup (nearly all Louisiana males over the age of eight have a gun, or access to one at all times), then went over to crouch by the back deck, squinted, looked, squinted again…he didn't see any snake, but since it was dark under the house and the snake was black, "Well, ma'am, could be I jes' don' see it."

"Well, *yeah,* I guess not. Thanks for coming over with the gun and um… how long are you going to be working next door today?"

"Not fer long, ma'am," he said, and then he recommended I buy boxes of mothballs and sprinkle the contents under the deck, especially where I had seen the snake go under, near the back stairs. "Snakes don't like them mothball smells," I was informed.

So I ran to the Walmart and bought four big boxes of mothballs, which I could smell even before I opened the box, yuch. I left them in the bag on the back deck for Husband to spread, of course, when he got home.

I never saw that particular snake again, but I have no idea if it was the mothballs that drove it away or not. I do know that they smelled so badly, it kept *all* of us away from the back stairs and back door. You literally could not breathe for the fumes coming off those fuzzy little white balls, it took a month for the smell to go away.

That snake probably moved farther under the house, dug a new apartment and was settled in under the middle deck steps, for all I know.

It wasn't the last snake I saw in Louisiana, though, not by a long shot...

LITTLE SNAKES
ARE ICKY, TOO

In the summer of 2005, before we were hit by Hurricane Rita, we had an above ground pool installed off the back of the house. This pool was a large one, and it required the ground to be leveled, which left lots of big dirt piles sitting around the yard once more.

One pile was located next to the section of a new deck being built around the pool, which was going to connect to the existing older deck. In the course of landscaping and getting rid of these piles of dirt, workers uncovered dozens of little snakes, which they called "pygmy rattlers". These came spilling out in all directions after they apparently hit some sort of nest. At first I thought it was a nest of baby garter snakes, since I had never heard of pygmy rattlers.

I was interested and went back inside to do an internet search on this species, thinking to myself, well, at least they weren't baby water moccasins...

No, they weren't, but my search turned up something just as eye opening. Ground rattlers, or pygmy rattlesnakes, yes, they do exist and are found in Louisiana and obviously right in my back yard. I ran back outside to stand a cautious distance away from the edge of the deck, then called out to the workmen... were they *sure* what they had seen were pygmy rattlesnakes?

"Real shore, ma'am. See, we was watchin' one befo' lunch, tryin' ta wiggle down inta one of those crawfish mounds you gots all over yore yard? (I'll explain later) Got a good look at it, pygmy rattler, alright. Prolly been nestin' in that mounda dirt foh awhl, tho you doan usually see em dis close to a house."

"Did you see where all those snakes went to when you disturbed the nest?" I ask anxiously, scanning the ground, the deck, the spaces between the deck slats, my toes curling up off the boards as I do.

"Why, yes ma'am, we shore did. They all went straight unner yore deck, ever' last one. Funny thing, huh?"

Hysterical, oh yeah…. I'll start laughing once I go swallow a few tranquilizers…

WARNING: TOXIC SNOW

Southerners are funny about cold temperatures and snow. First off, you need to realize that in southern Louisiana, it can still be 70 degrees in November. December might be a little cooler, like 50 to 60, with some nights plummeting down to (gasp) 40 degrees or possibly plunging to (another gasp) *nearly freezing.*

Not zero, mind you. Just freezing. 32 degrees. When one of these rare, cold nights threaten the area, with even the merest glimmer of a possible possibility there might be ice or snow in the morning, the entire town goes on high alert. People frantically run to the grocery stores and jam the aisles of the Walmart, to make sure they have food in the house, especially bread n' milk, and firewood for the fireplaces.

On all the local news channels, the weather people look terribly serious and warn that school could be delayed or even canceled, and if you don't *have* to go out in the Killer Cold, for heaven's sake, do the sensible thing and stay indoors. You do *not* want to take chances with weather like this, they say in solemn tones.

There are dire little ticker-tape thingies running all day on the bottom of the television screen, urging you to CHECK ON YOUR ELDERLY NEIGHBORS...BRING ANIMALS INDOORS IF POSSIBLE...USE EXTRA CAUTION WHEN DRIVING...

As though a winter storm of historic, unimaginably vicious intensity was about to sweep down and entomb the entire town in ice.

The first time I witnessed the public panic over some possible cold temperatures, my response was something like... *Huh?*

You see, we had lived in the Great Snowy Upper Midwest, where the wind chill plunged to 40 or 50 below zero, and caused the trees to crack open. For the 15 years before that, we had lived in the Great Snowy Northeast, where one year it snowed clear into the first week in June. I had called my mother on the phone to cry about it, since I'd planted flowers like a dummy, thinking that the snow was over for the year. It wasn't.

Check on your neighbors, don't go outside, what nonsense was this? The cold came and went and left one gazillionth of a millimeter layer of fragile, delicate ice coating on the ever-present wet spots on the sidewalks and streets. You could have coughed on it and it would have melted, if that paints a better picture.

Perhaps a dozen toxic snowflakes had been sighted by the ever vigilant news crews.

School was delayed for an hour until the dangerous ice melted. I drove my boys to school and watched them mingle with the other kids on the sidewalk, who were all shivering and shaking, bundled in layers of jackets, coats, hats, mittens, scarves, the whole schmeer. My guys wore only the school uniform, which consisted of long pants and a short sleeved polo shirt.

Mothers anxiously escorted the smaller children to safety in case they were Overcome With Cold, or had to possibly walk by some ice that hadn't fully melted. My boys got a lot of stares, as did I, clad only in a short sleeved t-shirt and jeans. The temperature gauge on my car read 52. I ignored the stares and drove home. About 30 minutes later, I received a phone call from a very nice, but very concerned elementary school principal.

"Surely," she said, "you realize the necessity of dressing young children appropriately for the winters here?" She had received several calls from mothers who had witnessed my boys entering the school… on *this* morning, of *all* mornings, during this dreadful cold spell, *with no jacket or coat on.*

I agreed they had no coats on, which she could not quite understand. "It's winter," she kept repeating, "It's winter out there."

"For *you* it's winter," I kept answering. "For us transplanted Northerners, this is a summer night. My kids don't even put a sweatshirt on until it's about 30 degrees. In their last school, the teachers didn't even let the kids inside to play during recess until the temperatures dropped below zero. Not 32... zero."

"*No* school," she insisted, "No teacher or principal would be so cruel to a child."

"Oh, we're very used to the cold," I re-assured the poor woman, but I took pity on her and made the boys wear sweaters to school in the mornings until the Louisiana winter ended in February.

HANDY HINTS ON OTHER STUFF

Fire ants are evil, vicious insects straight from the Bowels of Hell. Their sting is 20 times stronger than a wasps, and burns like a fire under your skin. There is no cure, and the pain lasts for weeks. These ants are tiny, black, and mean. Those little sandy mounds you will see on the ground all over down South? They are nests. *STAY AWAY.*

Alligators can and do bite you and don't mind eating you for lunch, either. Please do not get suckered in by the weirdo's on Discovery or Nature channels on TV, who state that these creatures are misunderstood or harmless. Alligators only do two things: they either eat you, or they don't. *STAY FAR, FAR AWAY.*

You can indeed fry an egg on the hood of your car in Louisiana in the late summer, when temperatures are at their hottest, but it's really hard to get it off afterwards, so don't be as stupid as I was when you try it. Be smart and fry it in a frying pan that's placed on the hood of your car.

LAST, BUT CERTAINLY NOT LEAST...

The three stories that come next are about events in Louisiana that stood out in my mind. Well, everything about the time down there stands out in my mind, but these three incidents are kind of related to each other, in that they all involved mini dramas around three different types of Louisiana critters.

You might read them and think afterwards, did she make these up, or did they actually happen?

Yes, they happened. Really.

You might ask, did these people actually say all that stuff? Well, who the heck recalls each and every word that they've spoken ten years ago? Conversations are verbatim in a whole lot of places; in others, the basics of what was said is absolutely there, as best as I could reconstruct it. Go with the flow, as my Mom used to say.

(Okay, I actually uttered a *lot* more profanity when some of this stuff happened... but I didn't want you thinking I was too bitchy, so I cleaned some of my curse words up, geeze. Sue me...)

OLD RATS AND NEW RATS

Rats are vermin. I don't care how many people keep the nasty creatures as pets and can bore you to tears with stories of their intelligence, playfulness, devotion, blah blah gag blah. They are still rodents with icky naked tails and feet, beady little eyes, and front teeth that never stop growing.

Until I moved to Louisiana, I had rarely seen a real live rat. Maybe in a pet store, sure, trying to appear all cute n' harmless, running on a wheel or burying themselves in soft cedar shavings. I knew better. I had rat history, you see.

The first time I ever officially saw a rat was when I was a child, living in Clark Air Force Base on the Philippine Islands. The air base isn't there anymore, incidentally. Mt. Pinatubo erupted on June 15, 1991 and destroyed it, after being inactive for 600 years. (This is also the birthday of my son, Chase, which if you knew him, you'd realize this event sort of matches his personality, but he's mentioned in different stories.) Where was I... oh, on the island, yes. I was about six years old and my little brother was about three. We were both in our pajamas, lying on our stomachs on the floor, watching television. Paladin: Have Gun, Will Travel, was playing. We weren't allowed to watch a lot of television except for a few programs at night. Mom approved of Westerns, and so did the Philippine government, they imported a lot of American westerns to their TV stations.

Our television was against the back wall of the living room. My mother was sitting on the couch behind us. I heard my little brother say, "Cat!"

I looked over about the same time that my mother let out a scream, which scared the *hell* out of me, for I had never in my life heard her do that. I only caught a glimpse of this big, dark thing walking slowly along the wall behind the television...

TV's were bulky structures that stood on stumpy little legs in those days.

Mom snatched my brother and me off the floor and ran into her bedroom, dropping us both on her bed. She crouched down on the floor and looked under the bed and the dresser, then tucked all the edges of the blankets under the mattress. We were told to stay there and *DON'T MOVE!*

She ran out of the room, slamming the door shut behind her and we did as we were told, we sat huddled together in the middle of the big bed and did not move. A minute later I could hear her yelling into the phone to my Dad to come home immediately, there was a big rat in the house.

Later, as this story was retold, I learned that my Dad had been down in the squadron building with a bunch of the other pilots and flier type guys, and they were all laughing after my Mom's call.

"She saw some damned mouse," I believe is close to what Dad had said. A few of the fellows decided to tag along with him on his way home, supposedly to give him moral support, but in reality, just to tease my Mom about getting so hysterical over a mouse.

Not too long afterward, I heard my Mother yelling, as my Dad and his entourage came in through the front door, that the rat had gone into the kitchen. I heard men laughing. I heard my Dad being a smart ass to my Mom. Then it got quiet, all the men must have been going into the kitchen. A few minutes later I heard my Dad yell, *"JEEZZUSSS GODDAMN KEERIST, IT'S A RAT!!!"*

There was suddenly a *lot* of shouting and banging and noise, and I just sat on the bed holding tightly to my little brother. My mother came running back into the bedroom, flinging the door open and then slamming it shut. She got on the bed and held us both.

My dad had apparently been in the kitchen with the guys looking for the mouse, when he was confronted by a very nasty wharf rat, about a foot long, from what I was told later. He told us he grabbed a broom and jumped on top of a kitchen chair, as his stalwart supporters fell all over themselves trying to get out of the kitchen.

Once safely out of the kitchen, they suddenly recalled that they were supposed to be Guys and charged back in to do battle with the giant rat, trying to hit it with chairs, pots, pans, anything they could. They made a tremendous racket and finally killed it. I never asked how and my mom didn't want to know. They carried it outdoors and called Rat Control, who came to take it away and set rat traps up all over our house.

They caught more huge rats as the weeks went by, ugly things with tails as long as their bodies. One was caught coming through a hole around the drainpipes under the sink. We were forbidden to open any cupboards, and Mom made my brother and me sleep in between her and Dad in their bed for a long, long time.

I had rat history, oh yes, I did.

So when we moved to Louisiana and I saw rats in the back yard, Husband should have believed me. Being a My Wife Overreacts Kind of Guy, he didn't.

He had a new job, this was a new state, so we did the sensible thing and didn't buy a house that first year, we rented one instead. It was in a nice neighborhood, we had nice neighbors and it was a decent little ranch style house. It had a beat up, but still standing, six foot tall wooden stockade fence around the whole back yard.

I put our gas barbecue grill on the long cement patio, which was right off the back door, bought chairs and a table at the Walmart and learned quickly that you can't sit outside very often to eat in the summertime in Louisiana, due to the high heat, intense humidity and multiple king-sized bugs. The grill didn't get used that first summer, and you'll know why in a minute or two.

I am sitting out on the patio... determined to get the heck out of the house and away from the endless stacks of cardboard boxes still waiting to be unpacked... idly gazing out into the yard, looking at the strange, tropical trees I didn't recognize... at the very large elephant ear plants growing next to the stockade fence... at the rats walking on top of those horizontal supports that are on the inside of the stockade fence panels.

Your brain just sort of registers these things as your eyes pass over them, it takes a second or two before it stops cold on the word, *rats*. Then, it just reverberates itself into your consciousness a few more times.

Rats? Rats?! *RATS??!!!*

Yes indeedy-do, folks, *rats*, walking along the fence right in my rented back yard, three of them. Not in a hurry and obviously at home there, they proceed to make it to the end of the support beam and then skitter onto an oddly shaped tree growing in the corner of the yard, jammed against the fence.

I skittered right into the house and called Husband, who sighed elaborately and said I was most likely tired from the move and/or unpacking too long, and had probably seen chipmunks. "Did you have your glasses on?"

"Yes," I answered through gritted teeth, safely on the inside of the glass patio door, "I had my glasses on, and these weren't chipmunks, they were rats... brown rats."

"Chipmunks," he stated patiently, "are also brown, did you get a look at their tails?"

"Yes, naked, icky tails, because these were damn *RATS*, not chipmunks!"

I was informed that rats were nocturnal creatures and didn't normally come out much in the daytime, so he had no idea what I *thought* I had seen. Was I sure it wasn't some sort of squirrel? And he had to go back to work now and couldn't talk anymore.

His advice was to just not go out in the back yard right now. I didn't go out in the back yard the rest of that afternoon. I kept watch through the kitchen window off and on all day, and dammit, they were *out there.*

Rats, I tell you, rats, walked back and forth on those fence supports all freaking day long. They ran up into that weird tree, they ran down the tree, they scruffled around in the undergrowth at the bottom of the tree. Husband didn't come home until late at night, then stood out on the back porch and declared that he didn't see anything. (no duh, sweetheart)

This went on for a week. I made my two youngest sons sit out in the heat with me, to be my witnesses. "Do *you* see the rats?" I would ask them.

"Sure," they'd answer and point to whatever rat was visible at the moment in the yard or on the fence. They told me they had also seen them on the other side of the house, scuttling up and down onto the roof and running along the canopy which hung over the back patio. They helpfully pointed up at a spot which was directly over my head.

This is where you glance up so fast that you hurt your neck. Drag your boys indoors to once again, call Husband and demand that he *do something.*

He can't do anything, he is at work and can't do anything about some creature that he has never seen, he explains.

Husband makes it home early one night, and jokingly asks how many squirrels I saw today.

"Haha, you're a scream, honey," I answer.

He decides to barbecue. I follow him out onto the back patio, and watch as he takes the vinyl cover off of the barbecue (which hadn't been used yet that summer) and opens the lid.

He leaps backwards with a shout as a good sized brown rat and a baby rat leap out from the depths of the barbecue and plop-plop furrily onto the patio, then scurry off into the twilight.

Meanwhile, I've screamed and flung myself back into the house, slammed and locked the patio door behind me.

I catch my breath as Husband stamps all over the barbecue cover, in case more fugitive rats are hiding in there, then stare at him through the glass door as he jiggles the locked handle trying to get back into the house.

"How many chipmunks *was* that, honey?" I ask him as sweetly-nastily as I can manage, as he stares at me through the glass, "Or were they squirrels, baby?"

I unlock the door and let him inside. He doesn't say a word and goes to call an exterminator.

I tell him to throw out the grill. He says I am overreacting, but sensing that I am on the verge of some Emotional Thing that he doesn't even want to consider dealing with, he wisely rolls the rat-tainted grill to the curb that very evening.

Now, a lot of the workmen type people in southwest Louisiana are Cajuns. It would take too long to explain exactly what a Cajun is, but a true bayou Cajun will eat an alligator for dinner that he has caught in the bayou his house is built over. Yes, like on stilts. You can call exterminating companies and get a pleasant receptionist on the phone, sure, but the guy coming to your house is probably going to be a gator eating Cajun. They speak in a Southern drawl with a French accent. Wonderfully nice people, but they're a little… um… well, just read on.

The exterminator guy shows up in a white pickup truck. It has a cab section built over the truck bed with doors on the sides. He opens one of the doors and takes out a lot of cardboard tubes, with sticky stuff on the insides. He walks around to the back yard and over to where we've been seeing the rats, and starts to place the cardboard tubes along the support rails of the fence. These, he tells me, will mos' likely catch the rat I saw.

"Rats," I correct him. "Not one rat, *rats*. Lots of rats."

He adjusts a tube and tells me, "Thass not real likely, ma'am. If yew see one rat out in da daytime, moh likely mean deres bout a hunnert or moh yew doan see, dey live in cawl-uh-nees."

"I saw more than one rat," I repeat, "I see rats all day long, walking all over this fence and in this yard, multiple rats."

He turns to look at me and adjusts his hat. "Muss mean ya'll gots a few hunnert or mebbe a t'ousand roun' heah somewhere close, ma'am. Gonna be real mess on yore hans if dats da case."

He drives off in his truck and leaves me standing there, staring at the cardboard tubes, as my mind repeats over and over... hunnerts... er... hundreds?

The tubes do not work, the rats are smart and just walk around them or over them. None of the rats are dumb enough to see a sticky rat catching tube and walk into it, gosh no. The tubes stay in place for about a week, until they get rained upon and soggy, or squashed flat by the rats walking over them, causing the tubes to stick together from the sticky stuff inside.

I call the exterminator guy again and ask for some better traps. He drives back out in his truck with bait traps, which he fills with peanut butter flavored rat poison. I am ordered to keep my two small dogs indoors, as dogs love the taste of this stuff. "Bes' if yew keep yore boys in, too, boys'll eat a lotta stuff dey shun't," he instructs me. So I keep mah dogs n' boys in.

The smart rats get stupid, to my surprise, and eat the peanut butter poison. They start dying in stages, all over the lawn, one by one. They get disoriented, they stagger, they crawl along the fence supports only to start wobbling and then fall off into the growth below.

I don't allow the boys out into the yard at all.

I find it hard to even *look* out into the yard. No matter, the twins keep me informed about the ongoing ratocide by descriptive commentary when they are in observation mode, their faces plastered to the glass on the back patio door.

Kid One: Mom... Mom... you gotta see this... one just fell out of the tree.

Kid Two: Where? Where? Did you see it land?

Kid One: Right there. It landed all crooked. There's its head, see it wiggle?

Mom: Alright, I don't think you should be watching that. Get away from the door.

Kid One: Look! Mom, are you looking? I bet its only half poisoned, that's why it's still moving.

Kid Two: How can it be *half* poisoned, you moron? It ate the bait, that's why it's acting like that. It's just not dying fast enough, that's all.

Kid One: If it only ate a *little* of the bait, it might not die, jerk face. That's half poisoned.

Kid Two: It's totally poisoned. You're just stupid and don't understand. Mom, tell him he's stupid and doesn't understand.

Mom: Both of you get away from that door. Now.

Kid One: Five more minutes. I wanta see if it gets closer, first. Think it'll puke or have gross stuff leak out of its body somewhere when it dies?

Kid Two: You're so dumb. You're just so dumb, the last ones didn't do that.

Kid One: We weren't close enough, Mr. Know It All, so how do *you* know?

Kid Two: Mom, can we go out in the yard and get closer to this one? I think it's almost dead.

Mom: Don't you two *DARE* go out in that yard! And get away from that door!

I dial the exterminator and tell him for God's sake, to get over here and start picking up these dead rats, I have children here. "Ah'll git to ya when Ah can," he says. "Lotsa people got lotsa daid rats dis month, ma'am. Do yew know how minny yew gots?"

I tell him that there is no way in hell that I am going out there and get a body count. He finds this very funny and laughs. I hang up the phone and announce he is weird.

Finally the white truck pulls up into my driveway. I stand next to the garage and wait as he gets out. The boys are down to the truck in a flash, asking if they can watch him pick up the dead rats. "Why, shore," he says, smiling at them.

"NO," I pronounce, giving them the evil mother eye and ordering them away from the truck. They back up about three inches. "Oh, ma'am," says the exterminator, "Dem rats ain't gonna be in no shape ta do nuthin' ta dose boys. Let em come wid me."

"You just go get the rats," I tell him, looking stern and crossing my arms over my chest. So he takes a cardboard box from the front seat and walks around to the back yard. The boys race back into the house so that they can watch what happens through the glass patio door. I go in to watch, too, but not quite as enthusiastically.

I mean, you watch some guy walk all over your yard, picking up dead rats by their tails… your arms fold around yourself and your chin sinks lower and lower on your chest. It's just so grossly yucky, you can't help it. The boys poke each other as he gets to the rat that was the subject of so much debate earlier this afternoon.

Kid One: Saw it move, bet it isn't even gonna die. Shoulda been dead by now.

Kid Two: He picked it up by the tail, of course it moved, dummy. You're dumber than you were this afternoon. Mom, isn't he dumber than he was this afternoon?

Mom doesn't get a chance to answer, apparently the man retrieved all the dead-for-now-rats and is walking out of the yard, back to his truck. The boys tear out of the house and stampede down the driveway to escort him back.

I run after them, shouting for them to get back in the house this *instant,* stopping about 20 feet away from the man and his vermin filled box.

He's opened a different door on the back of the truck bed thingie, and has taken out some large, white, paper-looking squares. He places them on the driveway, then reaches into the box, lifts a poisoned rat by its tail and then drops it on the paper square, *splat.*

"*What* in God's name are you *doing!*" I shriek, my hands flying up to my face.

He looks at me. "Ahm stickin' da rats to dis trappin' paper, ma'am. Dey a lot like dose sticky tubes, on'y stronger. Cain't hev em rollin' roun in da truck when Ah drives, too hard ta git em out latuh. Dis keeps em in one place, till deys all da way daid."

"All the way de… all the way *dead?* Boys! Get back here this second!"

They stay right where they are, the little creeps, knowing full well that I am not about to go one step closer to what's going on. The exterminator is smiling and talking to them as the rats go splat onto the sticky paper. Seven, for this round.

My hands have crept from my cheeks to my temples, as I stand there, pressing them in on my skull and thinking… *oh god oh god I cannot believe I am standing here watching this why did we ever move here oh god ohhh god…*

He finishes and tosses the now empty box back through the window of the truck to land on the front seat. *Yuck.* He then picks up a sticky, rat encrusted paper by the corners and tips it into the opened door on the side of the truck bed thingie. I cover my ears, not wanting to hear it land. He picks up another paper, tips it in.

My boys are standing on each side of him, and after the last paper full o' rats is tipped in, they crowd close to the opening and practically stick their whole head in there. I scrunch my eyes shut and just shriek at them.

"Will you for *GOD'S SAKE*, get *AWAY* from that *TRUCK!!!* Get your *FACES* out of there!!!"

The man is scribbling on a clipboard. "Why, ma'am, I tink deys jes tryin' ta see dat big ole rat dats in dere. One Ah gots from da last place Ah wuz at."

"Big ole... *what* big ole rat? Bigger than the ones I just saw? BOYS!!!"

"Oh, it not goin' anywheres. All stuck up on dat paper. Good size rat, prolly go poun' and a half, two poun' at least. It prolly mosly daid by now, anyways. Yew boys wanta see?"

The blond demons hop up and down madly. Yes! Yes! Yes! They exclaim in delight, as I take a few steps forward, determined to smack the both of them in the head... maybe I'll smack the exterminator, too.

Into the truck bed thingie door goes the exterminator's hand, and out it comes, holding a sticky paper that has a fat, furry brown rat splayed out on it grotesquely, at awful angles. My rat phobia overcomes me at last and I stop dead in my tracks, watching in horrified fascination as he shakes the paper and the stickied-up rat, *writhes on it.*

I start looking around for something to throw at the exterminator guy. Preferably something hard. His radar must have been tuned in to the waves of the impending destruction I was unmistakably flinging at him, because he picks up the paper and tosses the unspeakable object back into the hole from whence it came, then shuts and latches the door. The boys groan in unison.

He tears a copy of the bill off his clipboard and wisely hands it to one of the boys to bring back to me, and winks at them. *Humor her, she's jes' a sissy girl,* that wink says.

They trudge morosely back up the driveway, giving me baleful looks that say plain as day, you-never-let-us-do-anything-cool, hand me the paper and then disappear into the house.

The exterminator and I stand and stare at each other for a few seconds.

"Yew not from roun' heah... are ya?" he says, turning to climb into his truck.

I make a face at him and his truck, then turn to go into the house so I can take a long, long, hothothot shower. When I'm finished, I sit down with a newspaper and start the search for a new rental house. Ah cain't face da sight of mebbe hunnerts moh mos'ly daid rats on mah lawn. Dey done won da Rat War, yup.

THINGS THAT GO SWOOSH IN THE NIGHT

In our third year of living in Louisiana, I had become tired of living in other people's houses and told Husband that we needed our own home. We liked it down here, I said, it's nice and warm, if a bit extreme as far as the bugs and a few other things went. We could always use it as a winter home if we ever moved back up North, right?

I search diligently online, call all the real estate companies and embark on the Hunt For A House. Within three days of searching over eight hours a day, and wearing out several real estate ladies, I have narrowed the search down to three houses. Husband has shown no interest in this endeavor whatsoever, and tells me to just let him know when I am down to a reasonable number of places to look at. He has to work, you know.

I drag him out to the three houses one afternoon. Of course, he falls in love with my least favorite of the three; a huge, contemporary concrete monster painted all in white, composed of three big square sections, with glass along the entire back of the house. It is situated on two large waterfront lots (which is why I had included it, he had mumbled something about water and fishing), has a dock and a boat slip. He *has* to have this house. I tell him it reminds me of Alcatraz, but he doesn't see the humor.

So we buy this big, industrial looking cement house (sigh) which stands on dozens of four foot tall concrete pillars. This is in case the bayou floods, I am informed by the real estate lady, which it can do every time it rains. Lovely.

It's an expensive, old neighborhood, and the police patrol it at least a half dozen times a day. Quiet. Thousands of trees.

Landscaped yards. Neighbors stop by here and there to welcome us, invite us to dinner or bring us food.

Living on the bayou is very different from living in the rental houses, which were located in the middle of regular landlocked neighborhoods. Tropical birds are everywhere here, most of which I had never seen before, except in a zoo or on television. Cranes, egrets, pelicans... one elegantly slender blue heron that picks its way delicately along the water's edge every morning, looking for fish. There are ducks and geese of all types and silvery fish that leap right up out of the water, then fall back with a splash.

The boys are on the dock fishing all the time, hauling in various species of little fish that they examine and then throw back. They catch shrimp in minnow traps, it's all very down-home-country sort of stuff. Husband beams at them down on the dock and then starts talking about getting a boat. I squint down at the dock, a hand raised over my eyes in the blazing Louisiana sunshine, wondering what that ripple just was in the water.

"Current," I am told.

"That's all mud in there," I answer Husband back, staring at the chocolate brown water that looks as though you could walk across it. I don't recall learning in science class that mud has a current, but then again, this is Louisiana, and deres strange things... er... there's stranger things that have happened.

I start to unpack cardboard boxes from the move. The boys settle in to school and the neighborhood. Husband goes to work and comes home late at night to stare at the bayou in the moonlight. "We'll build a new dock," he says, "and a new walk leading right up to the house. It'll be cool."

"Yeah, cool," I tell him, reminding him how the dock becomes completely submerged every time it rains more than three hours. "Let's spend a ton of money on something that will be underwater at least, oh... 65% of the year."

"We'll build a new seawall, too," he says, waving an arm at the entire back yard, "It will keep the water behind it. We can bring in tons of dirt, build the whole length of it up."

I just stare at him, then stare at the 309 feet of waterfront... estimated price for a seawall at $100 a foot, no less. *Right*, dear. Then I go back inside to unpack more boxes.

Eventually the boys start bringing a few kids over to visit at the house, friends from school. One has to get dropped off by his mom since he lives so far out, we'll call him Tommy.

Tommy's mom is Miss Lorna, a very pleasant Southern lady who drops her kid off and several hours later picks him up, at least three times a week. She usually has at least four or five other kids in her car, and one day after Tommy knocks at my back door, Miss Lorna is standing there, too.

"Hey, ah only hev a minnit," she says. "Tommy jus' loves it heah wid yore boys. Did ya'll realize dere's a big ole gatah in da yard?"

I did a sort of head shake, stared blankly at her and uttered something like, "Huh? Gatah?"

"Yayus," she nods and walks over to the railing on the back deck, which gives you a great view of the Hershey chocolate colored water we just paid a whole lot of money for. She points down to the corner of the yard, to an area directly opposite the dock near the water, and asks if I see it.

I lean on the railing, squint and stare, not sure if I actually manage to spot a "gatah", that my Northern-bred mind will even recognize whatever it is that's down there. I add a slight frown to the squint and tell her I am sorry, but I just don't see anything.

"Ya'll need to come see," she says, "So ya'll kin check wunce in awahl, make shore it's gawn, ya'll doan wan' the boys down thayuh neah da watuh, not if deres a gatah roun, not safe."

She says this as we leave the deck and start to walk down the driveway, and down towards the gently sloping boat slip that ends in the mudwater. I stop walking at the words "not safe".

I frown more and stare harder, my mind trying to shift into Weezy-anna speak.

Gatah. Gatah. Not safe, a gatah is not safe. Killer bird? Some weird sort of attack turtle they have down here? *Snake!* I knew I saw a damned ripple!

It's not a snake. It's not a turtle. It's not a mutant bird with teeth.

It's an alligator. An *alligator.* On my lawn.

My lawn, not properly in a natural habitat (like behind thick steel bars in the reptile section of a zoo), it's on *my lawn.*

I do an abrupt about face and speed walk back up the boat slip and safely into the garage, as Miss Lorna follows, talking the entire time. The kids in her car poke their heads out of the car windows, grin, and call out to the funny Northern lady (me), things like:

"Did ya'll see da gatah? Can ya smell it? They git big enuff, dey kin eatcha, didja know?"

No, kids, I sure didn't know… my, my, my, how clever and helpful you are.

Miss Lorna fills my stunned brain with all sorts of useful little tidbits bout livin' on da bayou. (doan go danglin' yore feet in da watuh… doan go walkin' neah dat watuh, speshully at night… doan evah stick yore hand in inny plant growin' by da watuh) — as I muster the nerve to come back out of the garage.

I stand behind the garbage cans and stare at the 20th century descendant of some prehistoric surely-Northern-people-eating dinosaur sunning itself in my back yard. Miss Lorna says she has to go now, nice to meetcha, and she stuffs kid heads back inside her car windows and drives off, waving.

I stand there and stare down the 30 foot boat slip to where the alligator peacefully basks in the sun. Then I go inside to scream up the stairs to the boys, *"DO NOT LEAVE THIS HOUSE FOR ANY REASON!"* and go to call Husband.

He is at work, where he always is, and very busy, which he always is. "You couldn't have seen an alligator," he says. "They're nocturnal and are actually quite afraid of humans. It's highly unlikely one would be there in the daytime, especially with people around."

I roll my eyes and remind him of how the chipmunk-squirrels turned out to be real rats, which he hadn't believed me about, either.

"That's neither here nor there," he says, "If you *did* see something on the lawn it probably *resembled* an alligator. Did you take a good look? How close were you?"

"What else in God's name resembles an alligator," I yell into the phone, "*Except an alligator?*" I tell him that I have witnesses, Louisiana people who know an alligator when they see one. He's never met Miss Lorna, he says, and doesn't know what sort of person she is and therefore, doesn't know if he can rely on her creature identifying abilities, either.

I get slightly testy, stating that I've been to the zoo numerous times, read a zillion nature books to the kids showing pictures of crocodiles and alligators, and watched countless hours of Animal Planet. "There's a damned big alligator on the lawn, and don't you *dare* ask me if I had my glasses on."

He can't talk anymore, he has to work. He'll look at it when he gets home. I hang up the phone with the slightest suggestion of a bang and call him a lot of names.

I check back and forth the rest of the afternoon on the gator. Sometime between the last check and running back to the internet searches on *alligator*, it disappears. A very thorough search of my backyard via binocular aided vision doesn't reveal it.

Whew. Maybe it was like a... a... swim-by visit.

On its way to wherever it usually hangs out, yeah... I ignore the internet information I had read all afternoon that keeps re-inserting itself into my brain... *territorial... keeps to the same area it's used to feeding in... can run amazingly fast on dry land...*

can leap out of the water in proportion to its body length… lurks under the water's surface, unseen, when stalking its prey…

Husband gets home, walks directly down the boat slip to stand at the edge of the muddy water and declares that he sees no alligator.

"No kidding, sweetheart, it's only about 9pm and the gator has been gone for hours. Unless, of course, it's lurking about two feet from you, right under the water you're standing next to."

"You are being an alarmist," he states, and strides back up the boat slip and into the house.

The alligator shows up on the lawn four more times that month. Twice, while the boys are fishing on the dock, it swims up and just floats right there in the water, watching them. I learn this only by hearing them complain one afternoon that it's scaring away the fish, hanging around like that.

"What's hanging around," I ask. "Oh, that stupid gator, Mom," they answer. "Almost got tangled in our line the other day."

Mom almost has cardiac arrest. "How far away," I utter weakly, sitting on a bar stool since my legs seem to have turned to jelly, "How far away was this thing from you?"

They tilt their heads and think a moment. "Well, today, if we had wanted to, we coulda reached over with the fishing poles and whacked it on the head. How far is that?"

I regain strength and leap off the bar stool, snatch up the phone and call Husband. In no uncertain terms I inform him, "Our sons have seen the alligator. It was less than three feet from them on the dock… *twice!*"

"It could have *killed them*," I yell into the phone, pacing back and forth. "You have to do something, I won't be able to let them out of the house! If you don't do *somethiiing*, I am going to pack my babies up (insert dramatic groans in duo here from my sons) and move them back up North, where there are no child-eating alligators!"

In a very patient tone of voice, since I am obviously distraught and illogical, Husband explains that he can't do anything about a creature that he has never seen. "Do the boys know for sure how big it was?"

"Big," they say, "Longer than the fishing pole, for sure."

Husband says "They're kids, what do they know."

I tell him the one that I keep seeing is big, too. "Impossible for you to verify," he says, "Since you won't get close enough to determine an accurate length. You're at a distance, honey, so naturally, it looks bigger than it really is."

He grudgingly concedes that it's probably an alligator that we've been seeing, but most likely a very small one.

A baby. A small, harmless, minding-its-own-business baby alligator. It probably just got curious about what the boys were doing and swam over to see. Ignore it, is his advice, it can't hurt anyone.

I bang the phone down and tell the boys that they are forbidden to go fishing on the dock anymore. I am beginning to hate the bayou and the creatures that may be lurking in its muddy depths… god only knows what else could be in there.

This goes on for two more weeks. Alligator swims around the dock. Alligator crawls up the boat slip and suns itself on the edge of the lawn. Since we've only been in this house since May, and it's now July, I begin to realize that this is probably the alligator's home stretch, and I just never noticed this on the real estate visits.

I mean, you're looking at the bedrooms, the kitchen, discussing the taxes and how much the utilities cost here… who would think to ask, while being shown *the lovely waterfront view*, "By the way, are there any man-eating alligators living in that dirty water over there?"

Husband and I have a fight about the alligator nearly every other night. He accuses me of making a big deal out of a baby alligator because in reality, I don't like the house he picked out.

We have come back from a night of shopping with the boys. Husband has purchased a new fishing pole and a large spotlight for night fishing, from the Super Walmart. We're arguing once more, because I am telling him there is no way in hell that my boys are going out on a dock at night to fish, not with that creature in the water.

In my anger, I forget the danger and march right down to the dock. Husband follows, toting the new pole and spotlight and calling to the boys to get their poles, everything is fine.

I yell back up to the boys that they better not do any such thing. I start shouting at Husband that this is *dangerous,* that the creature could leap right up out of the water and grab him or the boys, and we'd never find *any* of them! "No one," I repeat, *"No one is going to be night fishing on this dock!"*

The boys, of course, are halfway down the boat slip carrying their poles. I stomp off the dock and stand by the boat slip, about two feet from the water's edge. I've lost my temper entirely, along with the logical parts of my brain.

I yell loudly, not caring if the neighbors hear or what they think, that I am their Mother and that they are to *get right back into that house!*

I turn to glare at my Husband, waving my arms around at the dark water and shout that *this very minute,* that thing could be *watching* us, could be lurking *right here under the water* and we'd *never see it* until it was too late!

"Impossible," Husband states, setting down the pole and the spotlight, and then leaping off the deck to go and get his meal worms out of the truck. He pauses about four feet from me, then turns back around to say, "You're screaming far too loudly for anything to stay in the vicinity. Everyone knows that alligators are really more afraid of us, than we are of them."

Suddenly, there is a sort of slithery, sucking-swooshy sound and then a loud *splash* to my immediate right. Ripples of dark, muddy bayou water lap up the boat slip I am standing on and nearly reach my shoes, as I stand rooted to the spot, paralyzed by fear.

I feel Husbands hand close around my upper arm as he drags me back up the boat slip, clear to the top, next to the garage. He then lets go of me and races back down to the dock, grabs the spotlight, turns it on and shines the broad beam over the surface of the water. Even from where I am standing, I can see what looks like two small round golden lanterns under the water, right at the edge where the boat slip ends. It's the alligator.

Its eyes are glowing as the light hits them, almost exactly where I was standing just moments ago. It had to have been on the bank, no more than six feet from me, as I stood yelling and waving my arms around. It wasn't afraid of me, it stayed right there through my entire tirade. I am only lucky that it wasn't particularly hungry at the moment, or cranky enough to eat me, just to make me shut up.

Husband is shouting utterly stupid phrases like, "Look! It's an alligator! I see it! Do you see it, honey? It's right here!"

He starts walking along the bank, very close to the water's edge, and the small golden lanterns... follow him.

He tramps up and down the muddy (and slippery) bank at the water's edge and the lanterns follow his every move.

I regain a sense of reality (and also my temper) and scream at him, "For God's *sake*, stop being such a macho *idiot* and get away from the edge of the water!!!"

He ignores me and stands there on the wet, slippery bank, playing with the spotlight and the alligator lanterns.

"FINE," I shout furiously, "I'm not going to stand here and watch you get *EATEN!*" I drag the loudly protesting boys into the house with me and slam the door.

Neighbor lady comes over to see me the next day and asks what in the worl' was goin' awn last night?

I apologize for disturbing her and tell her what has been happening. "Bless yore heart, it's okay," she says, "Yore not use to sech things." She pats my arm and nods. "But you got yosef a nuisance gatah, souns like. Dey not sposed to be comin' up awn lawns and sech. You have to cawl the Wildlife Co-mish-uh-nuh."

She informs me that it's probably the same gatah everyone on the water has been seein' for bout three years now. They grow a foot in length every year, did I know that?

I know way more than I want to already.

I call the Wildlife Guy and he says I am on his list, since there's only one of him, and a whole lotta gatahs this time of year, ma'am. He shows up about a week later, a nice fellow in a big pickup truck. There's a lot of stuff in the truck bed that I presume is gator trapping gear. Ropes, sacks, duct tape, big hooks, more rope.

All of it smells. A lot.

He talks to me about what the boys and I have seen so far, as he fills out an official alligator complaint form. We walk down towards the dock. Okay, okay, I stop after about 20 feet and watch as *he* walks down onto the actual dock. He gazes up and down the long stretch of the bayou, then walks back to where I am standing and says he doesn't see a gatah right this minute, but that's okay. "We're gonna bait that tree by the water and see if we can't get it that way, ma'am."

Sure. Logical. I nod, finally, someone is doing something useful, like bait the tree. "Um… if the alligator is in the water, why are you baiting a tree? How do you bait a tree, anyway, what do you use?" I'm picturing a blocky sort of… well… block of something, set out by the water's edge, next to the tree where the alligator usually sits (lies?) near. Makes sense.

I follow the Gator Guy back to his smelly truck. He grabs a length of rope, one of the biggest metal hooks I've ever seen in my life with a stout ring on one end, and a dirty, lumpy sack with icky stuff caked on the outside. Has to be the alligator bait.

I make a scrinchy face at the smell emanating from the sack, and follow him back down the drive a bit, stopping as he continues down to a tree at the water's edge. He drops the sack on the ground, then threads the rope through the ring on the big hook, and ties it in a big knot. He tosses the hook over a low hanging branch on the tree and then kneels on the ground to untie the smelly sack.

He dumps out a big lump of… something… picks up the hook and *jams* the point into the… whatever it is… then stands up and hoists the lump over the water. He adjusts the rope up and down until the lump hangs about two feet off the surface, and then ties the free end of the rope to the trunk of the tree. Even from where I am standing, I can smell it, *beyond* gross in the hot, steamy summer air. He walks back up the boat slip, passes me and heads to his truck.

"What *is* that horrible *thing*," I mumble to him, holding my hands over my nose and mouth.

"Cow spleen," he says, tossing the sack back into the truck bed.

"I'm sorry, did you just say *cow* spleen? Like… an organ from a dead cow?"

He gives me an odd look and nods. "Well, it's only half a spleen, ma'am, but it shun't take much more'n half a spleen to get that gatahs attention. He'll smell that pretty quick and should go for it in a day or two."

"Go for it," I mumble stupidly from behind my hands, "You mean like… leap out of the water for it?"

"Oh, sure, they can leap straight up. If that's a four foot gatah you got in there, it can leap four feet out of the water. It'll swallow that spleen, swallow the hook… gatahs don't chew, ma'am, they just swallows… and then alls we gotta do is pull on the rope, and we got it. You just keep watch on that spleen, and when you see the rope under the water, means it's hooked. You call me."

Sure. Watch the spleen. Sure, I can do that.

He gets in the truck and drives off, leaving me standing there, taking tiny little breaths of stinky air from behind my hands and staring down at the cow spleen hanging from the tree.

I wonder, *why me.*

Two days go by. All I can do is stare at the cow spleen from the windows overlooking the bayou. I wash the dishes, run to the window.

Spleens there.

Throw in a loud of laundry, make the beds, run to the window. Spleens there.

Dash to the Walmart, worry about the spleen, dash home and…spleens there.

There has to be more to my existence than cow spleen observing, I think to myself on the third morning, hurrying to the window to check the spleen.

Cow spleen not there. The rope is still there, but it ends in the water. I speed dial the Gator Guy and he says fine, he'll be ovah sometime to haul that gatah up in the afta-noon, 'In the meantime, don't go down there and pull on that rope, ma'am."

Oh, gee, and I was planning on doing that as soon as I got dressed. I now stare at the rope as much as I stared at the cow spleen.

I take a shower, get dressed, make a cup of tea and stare out of the window at the calm bayou water, thinking…if I had swallowed a big sharp hook and half of a disgusting cow spleen, I surely would have let someone know about it. Where *is* that dratted creature, shouldn't it be doing something? Like… like… growling or stomping up on the bank to protest?

My back doorbell rings and I run to answer it. It's not the Gator Guy, but one of the Cajun painters I had contacted, who has come to give me an estimate on painting the exterior of the house. The Alcatraz white of the big concrete mausoleum is getting to me, it has to go.

He asks what the rope is on the tree, and I tell him, which taught me that very day that you do not *ever* tell a Cajun you have a gatah on a hook down in da bayou. He sprints down to the tree as I follow, yelling things at him like, "Hey! Where do you think you're going?"

He grabs the rope and starts pulling on it. Pulls and pulls, and I am now yelling, "HEY! WHAT DO YOU THINK YOU'RE...HEY!!!"

He gives a *big* pull and the steel hook (minus the spleen) splashily pops free from the water and lands on the lawn with a thump. Cajun painter inspects it, sighs a big sigh and comes back to where I am, shaking his head sadly.

"No gatah," he says. "Musta been a small wun, dey cain't swallow da whole hook. Prolly jus ever'ting else in dat swamp done et up dat spleen. Youse gonna hef to rebait it, but puhsonally, I pruffers a daid bird ta dem spleens."

I just stare at him and announce emphatically that I am *NOT* going to rebait a damned thing, and firmly refuse his generous offer to find me a dead bird.

Gator Guy drops by later and rebaits the hook with another smelly dead cow organ, agreeing with the Cajun painter guys assessment that it was mos likely a baby gatah that ate the previous spleen. "Keep watchin', ma'am."

The rope is back in the water by the very next morning, all taut, and it ends under my very own boat dock. Hmm...I carefully scan the water's surface with binoculars, but there isn't a ripple out of place.

I call the Gator Guy and he says he has a funeral to go to that afta-noon, and he can't be by until after that. Foh or five hours at least. He's in a suit, and he can't go haulin' up no gatah in his funeral suit. 'Sides, he hasn't got his truck or his gun. "Don't go near the rope," he repeats, and then asks if the Cajun painter guy is there today.

"No," I answer. "Oh, good," he says, "Cuz they like to take em and eat the tail. I don't want him messin' with that gatah, its state proppity now."

Eat the tail? Don't go near the rope? Gun?

God, what am I doing here and what's going to… I mean… I never thought about what happened at this stage. How *will* the Gator Guy de-gator my property, anyway?

I call Husband to tell him about the rope under our dock. He says that's nice, and then gives me a whole list of things that he forgot to take to work with him that morning, which I absolutely have to gather and bring down to him as soon as possible.

I go on this scavenger hunt as the boys wake up. They eat a healthy breakfast of Pepsi, cold leftover pizza and Doritos, in preparation for a busy morning of skate boarding. They've built a big wooden quarter pipe on our driveway, and are dying to try out the video camera their Dad bought them at the end of the school year.

I stand by the skate ramp and eye the distance between it and the boat dock. Hmm…probably should be safe…even if the gator gets mad and tries to run up on the boat slip, the rope isn't that long. I toss all of Husband's things in my car, and tell the boys sternly that I will be *right back*. *"Do not go near the water for any reason!"*

I am not content with the way they grin in response. "Get in the car," I order them. They look as dejected as can be and solemnly promise that they won't *do* anything, and aren't I *ever* going to trust them? I glare at them and repeat all the warnings out of my car window as I back out of the drive and see them wave at me in the rear view mirror.

I *speed* to the office, run in and dump all of Husbands stupid things on his desk, spend five useless minutes trying to convey what a serious event this is, and can't he at least come home until the Gator Guy gets there?

"Don't be silly, honey," he says, "You're perfectly safe. The gator guy will get there and take care of the whole thing. Stay in the house and make yourself some tea."

I make it back to my house in record time. The boys are skateboarding up and down the ramp, no one is eaten, no irate hook-laden gator is anywhere to be seen. Good. It's quiet.

Maybe I *will* make some hot tea and just try to relax.

Suddenly the boys are in my face with their video camera, holding it up for me to see, both talking at once. I don't hear a word they are saying, because my eyes are glued to the tiny image of what's obviously a very pissed off alligator, tossing itself out of the water right by the dock.

It thrashes back and forth, growling and making angry sounds, and then splashes back into the water. It does this over and over, as my mouth falls open wider and wider. I clutch the video camera in both hands and start running into the house, *I NEED THE GATOR GUY.*

He can't come. He's at the funeral. "Just let it alone, ma'am, it isn't goin' anywhere. Don't panic," he says, laughing.

Oh, screw you, I think, banging the phone down and dialing the 911. I reassure the operator that this isn't a people emergency, no one is dying or bleeding, but can they send an officer to please do something about this alligator?

I am holding the phone, its cord stretched out to the max, so that I can see through the window to the outside.

"We have boats on the bayou," I tell her. "We have boats pulling little kids on rafts, on this bayou. What if one gets caught on the rope, or gets too near to where the alligator is? This is a Louisiana creature, these are Louisiana policemen, can't they *do* something?"

The operator calmly tells me that this isn't their jurisdiction, it's Wildlife, and besides, there aren't enough officers to possibly take care of all the gatah calls they get. "Be patient and wait for the Gatah Guy," she counsels.

I call Husband to tell him that I've called the 911, and he must hurry home since the police won't come, and do something about this angry alligator. "I can't do anything," he says, "I have to work, and I'm pretty sure it's illegal for a civilian to shoot an alligator. You'll just have to wait for the gator guy. You should really try and relax, you'll get an ulcer, honey."

I wait for three hours. I replay the video a few times. I sit outside and watch the boys skate, not trusting that they won't venture down on the dock for a closer look. They laugh and skate and take bets on how much I might scream when the Gator Guy finally comes to take the gator away. One thinks that I could possibly faint, the other thinks I'll just hide in the house. The bets get bigger as the hours wear on. Finally, the Gator Guy pulls into the drive in his pickup truck. The boys show him the video. As he does a little paperwork and gets out a rifle to load, I get a lecture on gator capturing procedure.

First off, he wants it clear that he doesn't like pain in the ass conservationist types that go all to pieces when they realize, there's gonna be a dead gatah on their lawn soon. "Lil gatahs get relocated, three, foh feet, they still eatin' all that white type meat in the bayou... turtles, fish, things like that."

"Big gatahs have moved on to bigger prey or redder meat. Birds, dogs," he points to our two Shih-tzus walking around by the garage, "Gatah bait for sure," he says. "They'll eat cats that wander down to drink at the water's edge (I gulp, realizing perhaps that's why several of the semi-wild cats I rescued have disappeared) or people dumb enough to think gatahs won't eat you. Big gatahs get *shot*," he says.

"Usually it's Naw-therners, out-of-state folks," he says, while staring directly at me, "Who get hurt by gatahs, thinkin' they all harmless and stuff. Looz-ee-anna folks, they know better."

I inform him that one of my good friends up North that I've spoken to about this whole thing, is quite upset that this alligator might be killed, since he has read that they are relatively harmless if people would just leave them alone.

Gator Guy squints at me as he tucks the loaded rifle under his arm and says, "Well, ma'am, the gatahs, they can't *read* them books. They not harmless with a head fulla teeth, and they not swimmin' up to your boys in broad daylight to make friends. They're *huntin*.""

So I shut up.

The boys are quiet, filming him as he speaks, filming the gun he loads. As he strides down to the dock, the boys are in his wake, filming, ignoring my orders to come back this second.

He lays the rifle down on the dock, then lies flat on his stomach and actually scrooches forward until he is hanging over the water, nearly to his waist, and then he sticks his head *under* the dock.

I absolutely just lose it and run away, clear out into the middle of the lawn, sure that at any moment the alligator will leap up and snap this man's head clean off. I can't watch. I stand there with my hands up at my mouth and watch anyway, saying things like, *ohgod ohgod ohgod, please don't let there be a headless body lying on my dock with my boys filming it, ohhgod...*

He scoots around on the dock, peering under it. He grabs the rope and tugs on it. Tugs some more. Then he sticks his head up to shout, "It's right here!" He then spies me in the middle of the lawn and shouts, "Come here, ma'am."

"No," I shout back.

"Come *here*," he repeats, "You need to be here."

"I don't need to be there, *NO*," I shout.

"You come right up here on this dock, ma'am," he calls, "Or I'll get in the truck and leave."

I march, mad as can be, back across the lawn, down the boat slip and up onto the dock.

"Are you *CRAZY?*" I yell at him, stomping my foot with each word. The boys are laughing, filming this. He seems to find it all very funny, too, he's grinning.

"There's your gatah," he says, pointing over the edge of the water. "Come take a look at what's been causin' you all this worry n' fuss."

I edge carefully closer to the edge of the dock and peek over, as little as I dare. In a tangle of rope is this long, greenish-browny log looking thing. It's the top of the alligator's head. Something smells and I wonder if it's this tangled up creature. "Fine," I snap at the gator guy, pulling back from the edge of the dock. "*Now* what?"

"Why, we shoot it and haul it on up, ma'am." He stands up, picking up his rifle. "It's only a 22," he says, "Don't go gettin' all scared, ma'am." He holds it out to me as I stare at him, blankly. "Want to shoot it?" he asks.

The boys snicker and I can see the telephoto lens on the video camera extend towards me... ah, yes, let's get a close-up of Mom's face at this moment in history. The Gator Guy laughs at the look on my face, but before I can run away again, he puts the tip of the rifle directly on the base of the alligator's head and pulls the trigger.

BANG

He sets the rifle down and pulls on the rope, and I'm sorry, but this gator sure doesn't look dead, and what's more, it stinks. The big webbed feet with those horrendously long claws are making swimming motions, as the Gator Guy finally hauls the rest of it over the side of my dock and flops it down on the wooden boards. Oh, but it smells. It smells *badly*.

"Not to worry," he says as I back up and the boys crowd in, filming. "Shot it in the spine, it's not goin' anywhere."

Every fly in the state of Louisiana has descended on my dock and onto the nearly-dead alligator lying there. The smell is horrible, the flies are horrible, this sluggishly moving creature on my dock is horrible. I look at the Gator Guy who is busily unrolling a tape measure and decide he is horrible, too. The entire day and the entire event is horrible.

The gator is moving too much to be measured and tagged, so the Gator Guy picks up the rifle and shoots it again.

I am reassured that it's all dead now, and at some point, really, you can't react anymore. I just nod, dumbly, as my boys film the blood spurting out everywhere from the newest bullet hole.

Gator Guy presses me into service by handing me the end of the tape measure. I hold it, gingerly, on the end of the big tail as he stretches the gator out to its full length. He pronounces that it is six feet and eight inches long. Lord, does it smell.

"Good gatah," he says, smiling, "That's a damned good sized gatah you got there." He inspects whatever reptilian genitalia it has and announces it is male. He opens the jaws wide to measure them and asks if I want to stick my arm down there and get his hook back. He's grinning at me.

Har de har har, you shit head, I think.

He tags the six foot, eight inch creature that is now swarming with about three million buzzing flies, as the boys watch and film it. He then turns to the two of them and says that he is gonna need help draggin' the gatah back up to his truck.

Surprise, surprise, says their expressions, as the camera falters in their grasp. *Us,* touch that smelly dead alligator?

I take the camera and film them standing there, shifting back and forth on their feet. Oh, my, it's not funny when the tables are turned, is it, you camera wielding not-so-macho-after-all demons?

They refuse to touch the smelly dead creature.

I am forced to hand the camera back to them with the realization that if I don't help to drag this awful thing, it's going to be left here on my dock until the Gator Guy can come back with help. No, no and NO.

I sigh in resignation and look to the Gator Guy for instructions. He has hefted the dead alligator up and grabbed it around the chest, under the front legs, leaving one big webbed foot dangling. He takes the dangling claw thing and waves it at me. "It *wants* you," he says, grinning.

I wonder if it illegal to shove an official Wildlife guy into the bayou… then grasp the big claw in my hands as the boys zoom in, filming, their artistic sense restored now that Mom is once again film fodder.

We *pulll* and *pulll* and finally get it moving, drag it off the dock and onto the grass, then pull it up the sloping boat slip to the driveway. It leaks something smelly and disgusting all the way up onto the cement. The boys film it, of course, as they film me muttering things and coughing at the overwhelming smell.

We drag it to the back of the pickup and there, I realize, helping to drag a several hundred pound alligator is one thing, actually attempting to lift it up inside a truck bed is quite another. I have my limits, I can't do it. I don't have the strength. I threaten the boys and finally they hand over the camera, make faces at the smell and the fact that they actually have to touch this thing.

They grab the huge tail, the Gator Guy grabs the middle, and the three of them heave it up and into the back of the truck. They slide it to the very top of the bed, but it's still too long, so they have to curl the tail around in order for the tailgate to close. The boys then take turns filming each other poking the dead gator with their finger, as the Gator Guy goes back down to get his rifle, then comes back to finish paperwork.

I stand there and just stare at this massive thing in the back of the truck. The neighbor across the street gets home and walks across to see what's going on. He peers over the edge of the truck and gets wide eyed. "Dang big gator," he says, "Must be the one the neighbors have seen for years, feeding in this stretch of bayou."

He smiles and tells me cheerily since this big one is gone, another will soon move into its place. Territorial, you know.

He walks back across the street. I watch him walk away in his perfectly clean business suit and then into his house, as I stand there covered in dead alligator goo.

I turn back to stare at the alligator curled up in the truck bed. I stare at the huge webbed feet, studded with real claws. It has actual armor covering its body, with ridges all along the spine, like some sort of dragon you'd see in a movie. The tail is nothing but solid muscle; I've been informed that it can break bones if you get whacked with one. I've never seen a real predator this close, never touched one or anything. Discovery Channel or Animal Planet never tells you how ghastly they smell. It's menacing, even in death. I look out at the bayou and wonder…what next… *sigh…*

The Gator Guy has me sign a lot of papers, tells me it's been nice to meet me and he hopes that I don't have any more problems. He has to go get a gatah out of a culvert in back of the university, it's botherin' the teachers n' all, bein' there. Call him if I need him.

He waves and drives off with the dead alligator, and I am terribly happy to see them both leave.

I drag the hose down to the dock and spray off all the blood and flies. I spray off the mess along the length of the driveway, then trudge tiredly into the house and take a longlonglong hothothot shower.

Husband eventually gets home to ask how my day was, as he sorts through the mail. I tell him that a television news crew happened to be driving by as the gator drama was unfolding, and they captured it all on video. I am the lead-in story for the night on CNN.

"That's nice," he says, and goes into the bedroom to change his clothes. The boys hook up the video camera to our big screen TV, and later in the evening, we all settle down to watch the short film documentary, Mom and the Alligator.

Husband critiques their film and interjects comments on their techniques.

"You shouldn't have jiggled the camera so much."

"The angle is wrong for that shot."

"Next time, zoom in slower, the effect will be better."

The boys laugh all over again at the sight of Mom shrieking and running away on film. Mom just watches as the film rolls on and wonders why her ass looks so big when she knows for *certain,* that's a size ten skirt she's wearing. Hmm…

Mom also realizes how many bad words she uttered during the making of this film, most of which she does not recall using. Husband makes a comment that we probably won't be sending this to America's Funniest Home Videos, since lots of little kids watch that show. Mom thinks he is absolutely correct, there is no way in hell I am letting anyone think that my ass is that big.

The boys showed that film to all their friends, and to family when they visited one summer, and they all agreed I was funny and that the boys jiggled the camera too much. That film hung around for a while and then got lost when we moved. I don't miss it, because all the details are etched forever in my mind. I just hope as time goes on, the detail of my seemingly large ass fades and gets smaller.

Ah, life in Louisiana. Can it possibly get any better than this?

SNAKES AND
SALAD TONGS

Life in Louisiana wasn't all a Wild Kingdom episode. I didn't have to deal with giant man-eating creatures every month. Sometimes there were smaller creatures, like tree roaches, fire ants, or giant centipedes to do battle with.

Or snakes. There are lots of snakes in Louisiana, and at least five types are deadly poisonous. This tale is about one snake that I only saw for moments while it was still in one piece. Read on, you'll understand.

As I may have mentioned, our new house was a big, white, contemporary structure. Huge concrete squares, one stuck next to the other. Very stark, very tall, very forbidding, it resembled a prison or a fortress of some sort. Alcatraz, I nicknamed it. Husband got tired of me calling it that, so he gave into my numerous complaints and agreed to let me have it painted a color more in line with civilians living there, not inmates. I started calling painters to get estimates and finally hired two Cajun painters, who happened to be brothers.

The infamous alligator that had kept us away from the fishing dock has been dead n' gone for about a month, and I have reluctantly allowed the boys to resume fishing off the dock. I keep a watchful maternal eye peeled for any replacement alligator that may have heard about the vacancy we had.

Husband has bought the boys a new minnow trap, which they keep in the water, tied to one of the wooden dock posts. They haul it up several times a day to inspect what has wandered in and gotten caught. The bayou has brackish water, which is fresh and salt waters sort of mixed together. The minnow trap gathers little fishies, and... the bayou water being slightly salty... little shrimp, as well. These make great bait, I am informed, as the boys triumphantly flourish them about three inches from my face.

"Yeah, wonderful," I say, "And they smell. Put them back in the water, guys."

One morning, I am observing the boys through the wide glass windows of the great room for a moment, as they are down on the dock. They are kneeling by the minnow cage and poking at it with a stick or something. I can see they're sort of excited. Must be a lot of shrimp in there today, I think, smiling.

They look up and see me standing at the window, watching them, so I wave. They move quickly to kneel side by side, forming a solid shield of boy in front of the minnow trap, and then wave back at me in tandem. I am, of course, immediately suspicious and go out the door onto the back deck.

I stand at the railing and call out to them, "Hey, whatcha got in the minnow trap this morning that's so interesting?"

"Nothing," they say, still forming the boy-shield between my eyes and the minnow trap.

Nothing, which means that they have something in there they were poking that they don't want me to see. Better not be some poor turtle, I think, going down the steps of the deck.

I start walking across the lawn towards the dock to see for myself. They see me coming and hastily shove the minnow trap off the side of the dock, picking up their poles to resume fishing, as though nothing has happened. Hmm, I think, stepping up onto the dock, what in the world can they have in there?

"Hey guys," I smilingly greet them, looking over the side of the dock into the murky water. "What's in the minnow trap, can I see?"

"*Wellll,*" they say, "Um…you might not want to see. You're just going to get upset, Mom."

I frown, hearing these words, and back up a step or two… reassuring myself that it can't possibly be another alligator, and even if it is, it would have to be so tiny to fit into that trap, it would be a new baby, just hatched.

I snap my head up, searching the water frantically for signs of an enraged mother alligator... like the mommy T-Rex in Jurassic Park when she discovers the baby T-Rex egg is missing.

They read my mind and say, "Oh, *Mom*, don't be silly, there aren't any alligators around anymore, just the gar fish that sorta look like alligators. It's only a snake, here, we'll show you."

Hearing "*only a snake*" is enough to get my adrenalin pumps going. I leap backwards off the dock and onto the grassy area next to it, as they reach for the wet rope hanging over the side. I shout, "Don't you *dare* pull that up, *DO YOU HEAR ME?!* "

Too late, they've pulled the dripping minnow cage up over the side, dropped it with a sloshy thunk and now it rocks slightly back and forth on the dock, water streaming out of the mesh sides. It's filled with a lot of stuff and...dear God, it *is* a snake!

A long, black snake... a water moccasin. It's wiggling sluggishly in the minnow cage, having apparently swum in, attracted by the numerous tiny fish and shrimp gathered at the bottom, but is now unable to swim back out. It's trapped. Can snakes drown? Surely if we just leave it in there and kick the cage back over into the water, the dreadful thing will eventually drown, right? I order the boys to take the fishing pole and push the minnow cage back into the water.

"Awww, Mom!" they chorus in protest, "Can't we just look at it for a while? We haven't seen one this close before!"

"Before? Be... BEFORE? Does this mean you've seen *more* of these snakes?"

They nudge each other into mutinous silence. The snake continues to wriggle, causing the minnow cage to gently roll back and forth, back and forth. I can't bring myself to look at it anymore, but I do glare at the silent pair and threaten them with dire consequences unless they tell me where they've obviously seen other snakes like this one.

Their eyes shift to my feet. I glance down, suddenly a bit uneasy. I had hopped off the dock and was now standing on the grassy bank that slopes sharply down into the water. There is a gap of about ten inches where the bank ends and the dock begins. It then drops off at a steep angle and lord only knows what's under there, in all the mud and goo and dirty water.

Enlightenment suddenly hits, and I defy the laws of physics and my own bodily limitations, by managing to leap both straight up into the air *and* backwards about four feet. I stand, trembling after I have landed, as they both look at me and say, "Yeah, we've been seeing them go in and out of that space a lot (that you were just standing next to, haha)." The boys nod and nod, "They're sposed to *attack* if you're near their nest, but so far none of them have."

They sigh. These dreadful children sound almost disappointed as I stand there, trying to get my knees and nerves under control. I've got to call Husband, I think, demand that he come home and do something about this poisonous reptile on the dock.

I sternly order the boys to get off the dock *this very second!* They throw down their fishing poles, scowling. "You treat us like *babies,*" they accuse me. "We didn't stick our *hands* down there or anything."

I turn around to walk back to the house, only to find myself face to face with the two Cajun painters, who heard all the yelling and fuss as they drove up and decided to come down and see what it was all about. "Thot we heered da word snake, ma'am."

I point toward the minnow trap. Which Was A Mistake. One I did not realize at the time, but the lesson is etched in my mind forever, believe me. The Cajun brothers clamber onto the dock and squat next to the minnow trap, bending over it. They say things like, yep, look at dat, and then they rock the trap back and forth sharply with their hands. I make protesting noises and they both look up at me and grin.

"Why, ma'am," they say, "ain' a ting ta be 'fraid of. Dat ole snake, he ain' goin' no where, he all stuck up in dat cage. Beside, he mosly daid."

"Mosly... you mean mostly? *Mostly* dead? How can something be *mostly* dead? It's either dead or it isn't dead, so which is it?"

"Lessee," he says, and then nods to his Brother Cajun, who deftly flips open the catch on the minnow trap and dumps the entire contents onto the dock. I scream and run back up the boat slip. Motherhood kicks in, I run back down, *my babies are on the dock with a poisonous snake...* sanity then over-rides motherhood and causes me to stop about ten feet away.

"GET OFF THE DOCK NOW! NOW! *NOW!*" I scream, feeling all the veins about to explode in my head and neck.

The Cajun brothers both wink and nod to the boys, "Go wif yore mama, she gonna bust," they say. The boys obediently trot off the dock and scowl at me again as they walk past.

Holding my hands to my face... I seem to be doing that a lot in Louisiana for some reason... I scrunch my eyes up and try to look only a little bit at the mess on the dock, which both brothers are leaning over, inspecting.

Nothing much seems to be moving, except the little fish flopping about and a few of the shrimp. The snake is just sort of lying there, but, I reason, it could be a trick. It could be pretending. I say this to the Cajun brothers and they nod without looking at me.

"Could be, ma'am... it still look mosly daid."

Then, without warning, one of them picks up the perhaps mosly dead water moccasin by the tail and stands up, holding it out at arm's length. He then shakes it back and forth.

I am too stunned to even move or yell at him, all I can think is that the snake is a *lot* longer than I thought it was... oh oh oh my... then the snake starts to wriggle.

The Cajun immediately drops it and then *stomps* on it near the head with one sneakered foot. He holds it there pinned to the dock, as both brothers grin at one another. "Hey now," they say, hands on their hips, laughing, "Dat ole snake is still a lil bit live!"

My hands have somehow crept to the top of my head and I am gripping my hair, terrified and unable to move… there's a poisonous snake under the sneaker of a crazy Cajun, only ten feet from me… what now, ohhh, what now…

The Cajun turns to look at me, he's still grinning. Tells me since he duzzn't hev his snake stompin' shews awn, he cain ackshully kill it, so he jes gonna grind it a lil.

"Grind it, absolutely… grind it… sure, that's what anyone would do while standing on a highly venomous reptile. When you leave your official snake-stomping shoes back home, I guess you gotta grind. Um… pardon me for asking, but if you had worn your other shoes, I'm guessing you wouldn't need to… grind?"

"Oho, no ma'am, then yew jes stomps on em, smash da haid right flat. Roons dat haid, tho. Dey makes a mighty nice hatband wid da haid awl in wun piece, ma'am. I been wantin' a hatband, mah cuzzin has wun. But it yore snake, yew wan I shudd grind it, I grind it."

"Well… well… will it be dead then? After a grind, is it dead? *All* the way dead?"

"Prolly cood be closeta daid, ma'am. Ony way ta git it *rilly* daid is put it back in dat minnow cage, let it drown.

Jes' check ever wunce in awahl, it be daid befo' long."

"NO… um… no, thank you, I don't want to keep testing it for deadness. Just… go ahead and make it as dead as you can." I nod and gesture at him, waving my hands—go forth and grind, the gesture says.

So he twists his sneaker back and forth and grinds the snake into the dock for a few moments, then lifts his foot to check. The other Cajun Brother bends down, peering at it. I continue to just stand there, hands back on my head, watching in horrified fascination.

After a squinty eyed investigation, they both pronounce it mosly daid, but decide there's only one way to be absolutely shore. So the Grinding Cajun brother once again picks up the questionably dead snake by the tail... the head is hanging all crookedy and awful to one side, *ech*... then he pulls his arm back, like he is going to pitch a baseball, and lets it fly forward.

I, of course, expect to see the entire snake go winging through the air and into the water... but instead, he holds onto the tail and just the snake's head flies off, high into the air. Up, up it goes. I scream and just about fall on my ass backing up from the sight of it circling and circling up there, then coming downdowndown fastfastfast and landing somewhere on the lawn.

In my shock and surprise, I didn't notice the exact latitude and longitude of the severed snake heads final resting place. Another Mistake. I am shaking all over with so many emotions and adrenalin at this point, it's a wonder that I can even breathe.

The snake's body is hanging from the Cajun painter's hand, dripping blood all over my dock. Headless, really dead, and now it won't even make a decent hatband. Dear God, what has happened to my brain.

He asks if I want the body and I shake my head numbly, no. He tosses it in a long arc out over the surface of the water. I watch the body wave lazily through the air and then land with a splash into the muddy water from whence it came.

The Cajun snake killing brothers shake their heads as they walk by me. I am coming out of my brain daze and scanning the lawn, trying to locate the snapped off snake head. I don't see it anywhere. "Hey, wait, where are you guys going? I don't see the head, did either of you see where the head landed?"

"Nope," they answer. "Oh, and ma'am, dose haids gots venom in dem still, jesta let yew know. Bes' if yew doan go barefoot foh awahl, yore boys, neether. Step on dat haid, step onna fang, poyzen getcha foh shore, ma'am."

Oh

Dear

God

A poisonous snake head full of venom is lying hidden in my lawn. I rush inside to call Husband at work, who becomes upset at the fact I let the Cajun painters do such a thing.

"How could you stand there and let them do such a thing?" he demands.

"How could I… how was I supposed to know what the hell they were going to do!" I shout back into the phone. "I didn't know they were going to *dump* the damned thing on the dock and then *stomp* on it!"

"You could have told them not to touch it. You could have taken the minnow trap away from them."

"Are you out of your *mind*? It happened so fast no one could have stopped it! And take the cage from them? *Touch a minnow cage with a live snake inside of it?*"

"You said it was mostly dead. Couldn't possibly have hurt you at that point."

"*They* said it was mostly dead, and what difference does it make? There is no way in hell I could have prevented this once he picked that snake up!"

"The fact remains that you let them kill the snake instead of telling them to put it back into the cage until I got home. Now we have a snake head in the lawn that possibly has venom in it. You're going to have to go out there and find it before someone steps on it."

"I told them to kill it, yes. I *never* told them to snap the damned head off! And I was upset, my natural instinct was to kill it. I didn't know the entire head would go flying off into the stratosphere! And *how* do you suggest I find it?"

"It has to be in the lawn somewhere. Go down by the dock. Make sure you wear thick shoes, and look around in the grass until you find it. Just pick it up and throw it in the bayou."

"Pick it up? With *what*, pray tell, do you pick up a decapitated venomous snake head with? And I am *not* going back down next to that dock, it's where the kids said they saw more water moccasins going in and out, there's probably a nest!"

"You're so negative. Why do you always have to be so negative? They're not going to bother you, just wear a big glove or something. How hard can it be to find one snake head?"

"Not going to be hard at all, because there is no way on this *earth* that I am going anywhere *near* that dock to find that head. Period."

"Fine. Let it sit there in the lawn with the venom intact in its fangs. Let some kid wander by and step on it, or the old lady next door. Fine. Let them be poisoned because you let the stupid painters snap its head off."

"I hate you. I absolutely hate you. This is not my fault, it's the *painters fault.*"

"You don't really hate me, you're just overly emotional at the moment."

"No, I really hate you."

"Fine. Call me when you find the head. I have to work."

We hang up and I really do hate him. This is not my fault, and damn him for knowing that Mother Guilt will eat at me, making me worry about the snake head lurking in the lawn, just waiting for some Innocent Person to step on it and become envenomed.

Big glove, right…*not*. Hmm, how do I pick up a snake head. I start to look through drawers in the kitchen at random, looking for inspiration. Big tined serving fork…oh, yuck, don't even picture skewering the damned thing. Wooden spoons…no, it could roll right off. Straws, measuring cups, salad tongs… hmm…

I hold them in my hand, visualizing it. They're metal tongs, almost ten inches long, yes, these could work. I'll find the head, throw it *and* the tongs right into the bayou, for there is no way I will ever allow those tongs in my house again.

Holding the doomed tongs and wearing thick, rubber soled gardening clogs, I make my way cautiously down to the probably-snake-infested-area. I step carefully, gingerly. I don't want to accidentally be standing *on* the crushed snake head and then have to toss the gardening clogs into the bayou along with the salad tongs, I like these clogs.

I find no sign of the head. Mentally, I divide the grass into grid sections and scan each one. Nothing. Grid by grid, I step ever so carefully, bravely poking the turf here and there with the end of the tongs, in case the head like, slid through the blades of grass or something.

Nothing. I widen my search, and then re-search the previous grids. It simply isn't there. Could it have landed in the water? No, I would have heard a splash, right? Could something have gobbled it up that quickly?

Stop it, you're just going to creep yourself out. And don't you dare imagine multiple pairs of snaky little eyes sizing you up from under the dock... *it'sss her... there she iss, the one that gave the go-ahead on the hit... she'ss alone... only armed with salad tongsssss...*

Yuckola to the max, I'm outta here. I'll simply post a big sign. WARNING...VENOMOUS SNAKE HEAD SOMEWHERE ON THIS LAWN... WALK AT YOUR OWN RISK!

Yeah, that should do it. I call my Husband to inform him that I performed a very thorough search of the entire Kill Zone, with state-of-the-art equipment, but was regretfully unsuccessful in my mission. "What's our course of action now, General?" I ask.

He asks if this is humor and I swear to him it is not, that I am simply in guerilla warfare mode, brought on by living in the midst of the Louisiana jungle. He finally catches on. "Cute, honey," he says.

He eventually gets home, takes a flashlight and the salad tongs, and searches the entire area again, down by the dock. He can't find the elusive snakes head, either. He theorizes that it was probably stomped so flat that it's unrecognizable, therefore it's possible that the fangs were snapped off, and the whole head could actually be harmless.

Either that, or I wasn't paying enough attention when this incident occurred, and the head in actuality is lying in the two feet of mud on the bottom of the bayou. His guess is that it's in the mud. I know it isn't, but it's a moot point by now.

He calls the Cajun painters and tells them in no uncertain terms what he feels about the snake incident, and that he certainly didn't appreciate them endangering the entire neighborhood that way. I cough and semi-glare at him, so he adds, "And my wife."

The painters say they unnerstan, acorse, and by da way, dey won' be back ta paint da house.

Sigh… nobody won today. The snake lost its head, the painters los' a hatband. Alcatraz isn't going to lose its industrial façade. Oh well.

At least I didn't have to throw my salad tongs in the bayou.

C'EST LA VIE

It was time to move on. Louisiana had been our home for four years, but life had other plans for us. Husband found a new job, we packed the house once more, the boys, the animals, my unused undergarments and said goodbye to the Deep South and the many friends we had made there.

Yes, living down South had been an adventure in many ways. I don't miss the heat, the humidity, super-sized bugs, fire ants, wild creatures, alligators, snakes, hurricanes, muddy water or the mold.

But I surely do miss the friendly, charming, and wonderful folks who live down there... wish I could have taken you all with me.

BOOK JACKET
DILEMMA

zeecee: Are you here?

Halliegirl: Yeah, what's up?

zeecee: I need you to read this and tell me what you think... just off the top of your head, don't think too hard

Halliegirl: Okay.

zeecee: Here is the controversial new work by a mysterious, unknown author. While some of the sections might amuse the reader, certain others may cause one to think, Jesus, this person is sick and in desperate need of therapy. If any mental health professionals reading this book recognize any of the fears, phobias, obsessions, or fetishes expressed in this book, we'd greatly appreciate it if you would contact us with the name of the client/ patient/inmate. We are dying to know if there are any additional twisted or highly disturbing episodes we could have access to. All replies will be held in strictest confidence.

zeecee: Well?

Halliegirl: Wait, I'm still reading. Okaaay, where did you get this?

zeecee: It's book jacket information... you know, like from the back of a book

Halliegirl: What the heck are you *reading*? Some book on abnormal psychology, or something? Serial killers? Homicidal maniacs?

zeecee: What? No! I wrote this! For my book!

Halliegirl: You wrote a book on fetishes and weird stuff?

zeecee: No, no, no, goofball, it's meant to be humorous... you know I can't stand stuffy and boring... I just didn't want what everyone else had, you know?

Halliegirl: Zee, it reads as though you're some highly crazed lunatic who has written a book on bizarro shit.

zeecee: Some of the stuff in my book *is* about bizarro shit, Hallie.

Halliegirl: Some of it is. Okay, lots of it is. But even so, you could scare people.

zeecee: Too much? I should tone it down? Take out fetish and disturbing and twisted?

Halliegirl: It needs a slightly less sinister tone.

zeecee: Less sinister... hmm... humorous, but not sinister...

Halliegirl: Or creepy or scary. Just write something funny.

zeecee: I have Humorous Writers Block... the funny is not flowing... I'm in a morbid frame of mind for some reason lately...

Halliegirl: You're just stressed. You have this book to get out, the move coming up, David won't pack anything, as usual. It's just stress.

zeecee: He rescued a beat up, filthy old broom from the trash pile yesterday... he keeps rescuing old things I throw out...

Halliegirl: Because it's David we're talking about, I won't even ask why.

zeecee: I pointed out we had 4 other brooms and the old one deserved a decent burial... I even offered to help send it to the afterlife...

Halliegirl: Which means you two had a fight over the broom and you threatened to set it on fire. I know you.

zeecee: It wasn't a *fight* fight, simply an intense verbal exchange... anyway, back to the book jacket...

Halliegirl: Send me everything you've written and I'll read it and tell you my thoughts. Is this new stuff or the stuff I read already?

zeecee: You read most of it... some of its new, but I'm sure you read about the gator and the snake and Sam's club...

Halliegirl: I did. Those are humorous stories, so you have to have a book jacket blurb that reflects the content of what you've written. You can't submit that other stuff for your book jacket, unless you plan on writing horror stories. Then it would fit.

zeecee: Horror stories... hmm...

Halliegirl: Oh God. Forget I said that. No horror stories, no horror stories! You're weird enough with the humor, I'm not sure I could handle what you'd find horrifying.

zeecee: Sniffling now and it's all your fault...

Halliegirl: You'll get over it. Look, why can't you just say something like, Here is a collection of tales that mothers can identify with—follow the antics of ZC and her brilliant, but eccentric Husband, and their 5 unconventional children as they——-something something, I don't know. In that vein, okay?

zeecee: Gawd... it makes me sound like a glicky June Cleaver or Brady Bunch mom... it's not *me*, Hal...

Halliegirl: Okay, Leave It To Beaver Mom, you're not. You know, I can't think of the Brady Bunch now without remembering the TV dad was gay.

zeecee: Gay guys are hot... and only 3 of my 5 kids are somewhat unconventional, the other 2 are nearly normal... oh, did I tell you Keith wants to minor in psychiatry in school?

Halliegirl: Nooooo! Reeeally? Goodness gracious ME, what a surprise! Who'd have ever thought of it, coming from one of *your* kids?

zeecee: Sarcasm... I definitely sense sarcasm...

Halliegirl: That's what friends are for.

zeecee: Okay, smart ass... so fine, fine, fine, I need to come up with a different book jacket blurb thingie...

Halliegirl: Message me when you come up with something *appropriate.*

zeecee: Yes, mom...

STUPID THINGS
I'VE DONE #1

I was in a crowded dressing room once, trying on new outfits. Came out of my little booth, so I could see myself in the big three way mirror at the end of the hall. I had to wait my turn, as there were a lot of women jockeying for position in front of that mirror. I finally got my turn to view the outfit from all angles, turned and went back down the hall, opened the dressing room door and walked right in on some half naked lady who shrieked at me. She had forgotten to lock the door, and I had forgotten which room I had been in. Obviously, this wasn't it.

❂

For some unknown reason, even though I can read both of the words PULL or PUSH on the doors of business establishments, my brain conks out at times and I stand there like an idiot, tugging furiously on a door that has PUSH OPEN clearly printed on it. Yes, I also perform the other half of that Stupid Action, I walk up to doors and push and push and then curse because it refuses to open, while other people walk past me and pull on the door with PULL OPEN marked on it. They always give me really strange looks.

❂

Having five kids can sometimes do weird things to your brain, and sadly, you don't even notice that this has happened... until you automatically reach over and proceed to cut up the meat of the person sitting next to you into tiny, bite-sized pieces. Only they're not one of your kids. And it's at a dinner party for some potential new partners that Husbands business hopes to impress, and maybe get them to sign a contract. At least the gentleman whose meat I diced up didn't ask to have his seat changed.

❂

After grocery shopping one afternoon, I tried to start my car and the key wouldn't work in the ignition. I tried it again and again, yet still it did not work, the car would not turn on. I went back into the store to ask if I could phone Husband to come get me (no cells phones back then), and one of the clerks asked if he could look at the car.

"Sure," I said, grateful for the help. So he gets in my car, inserts the key, turns it and the car starts. "That's weird," I said. "But before you go back in the store, let me try, okay?" He climbs out of the car and stands there as I get behind the wheel, stick the key in the ignition and try to start the car. It doesn't start.

"I don't *understand* this," I wail, smacking the steering wheel. "Why won't it work for *me?*"

The clerk reaches over, takes the key out of the ignition and says to me, "You're using the wrong key, ma'am. You're driving a Dodge and this here key you keep trying is labeled Ford."

Sure. I knew that.

I once spent the entire day searching diligently all over the damned house for my eyeglasses, which I later discovered on top of my head, having forgotten, obviously, that I had shoved them up there early that morning.

I woke up in the middle of the night once, needing to pee. Tired, so tired, but I pulled the covers back, got out of bed and managed to stumble into the bathroom. Plunked down on the seat, still mostly asleep and just functioning on autopilot. *Find Toilet, Sit and Pee.*

I did find the toilet, I did sit and pee. I did not, however, remember to pull down my pajama pants prior to plunking my ass down on the toilet, and therefore, peed right through the fabric. And was still so tired that I didn't realize what I'd done until I stood up, and finally noticed my soaking wet pajama pants clinging to my legs. I woke up after that.

Whenever I can't open a tight jar lid, I keep twisting and jerking until it gives way... but sometimes my hand accidentally loses its grip, flies up and smacks me in my own face, which is just so annoyingly stupid. After this happens, I usually continue to wrestle with the lid, but sometimes a lid just *refuses* to untwist, so not only are you irritated and in pain, you still can't access the insides of the damned jar.

While preparing dinner once, I got into a heated conversation with Husband over the phone. I became more and more upset as the conversation escalated into an argument, and at the end, found myself shouting something like, "*FINE!* You know for a *doctor,* you're *still* one of the stupidest men I know!"

Not until I had banged the phone down and taken a few deep breaths did I realize that while arguing, I had apparently been waving a big wooden spoon around in the air for emphasis on verbal points I had been trying to convey, and had thwacked spaghetti sauce all around the kitchen. Realizing that you've done this does nothing to help calm you down.

FAULT LINES

Side Note on Fault Lines — These little tales are so named because no matter what the incident is, or the circumstances surrounding it, or if I was even present at the time it happened, somehow always end up being My Fault.

FAULT LINES: JUST SIT DOWN

We are in a furniture store, shopping for a new couch. It's a large store with plenty of selection, and as I browse, I see several pieces right away that I like. Husband sits on each one and says that they aren't comfortable. I thought they felt just fine, but I continue to look around and soon find another couch. Husband says it has too many cushions and doesn't "feel right" when he tests it out.

I try various couches, loveseats, and even some oversized chairs. He vetoes them all, one by one. The upholstery or the fabric is too hard, too soft, too slippery, too ugly, too easily stained, too flowery, too girly, too patterned, too scratchy, too something.

There aren't enough cushions or there are too many. The seats are too high off the ground or too low to the ground. He claims none of the backs are high enough to support his head, and none of the couches are long enough to fit him if he decides to lie down.

He tests literally every piece in the store and doesn't like a single one.

As a last resort, I mention perhaps we should consider buying a large sectional couch, but he says no, they take up too much room and besides, he doesn't like any of them.

Frustrated and tired, I give up and walk out of the store, muttering, and climb into our truck. Husband follows, gets into the truck and starts it up. He turns to look at me and says, "I cannot believe that you couldn't pick out a new couch."

FAULT LINES: DON'T TREAD ON ME

I am in my late twenties. I'm barefoot, playing around on the lawn at my parent's house with their terrier mix, tossing green tennis balls to see how many he can possibly try to fit into his mouth at the same time. The grass is overly long because it's been raining, and hasn't quite dried out enough for my father to mow the lawn.

As I dance past the dog, teasing him with yet another tennis ball, I suddenly feel a terrible, searing pain in the heel of my right foot. In the next second, a wooden staff whips up out of the long grass and whacks me hard on the side of the head. The pain in my foot is so bad that I am gasping, trying to understand what just happened while trying not to fall over, because whatever stabbed me in the heel, is still stabbing me.

Holding my head with one hand and the wooden staff with the other, I take a deep breath, trying to calm down and keep my balance. Looking down, I realize I have stepped on a metal garden rake. Stepped on it barefoot, with all my weight, and as a result, several of the sharp metal tines have punctured deeply into the bottom of my heel. When I stepped on the tines, it made the rake handle come swiftly upright, and this is what has hit me in the head.

I hold the wooden handle securely and lean on it, taking a few more deep breaths...then, while pushing the rake tightly against the ground with both hands, I pull my injured foot *off* the metal tines, in one quick motion.

I sit abruptly on my ass on the long grass, and curl my leg around, lotus style, so I can see what my heel looks like. There are two symmetrical round red holes, oozing blood. The pain has begun to creep up my leg, an awful, heavy, dull-ache pain. I get up, and using the rake as a support staff, hobble over to the house and call for my mother. She helps me into the kitchen, where I telephone Husband. He is working in a big city hospital and fixing other injured people, so he cannot possibly come to my mother's house out in the suburbs, to tend to me. My mom drives me to the local emergency room, instead.

The ER people wince in sympathy when I explain what happened, and then wash out the round red holes with lots of sterile water. The tetanus shot I am given makes my arm hurt almost as much as the wounds on my heel, and my mother asks me what I am going to do now.

My three children are already at her house, as its summertime, school is out, and they are nearly always at her house for the entire summer. But I also have dogs to take care of, a Husband who is not home to deal with anything, ever, and my mother doesn't want my big dogs at her house, running all over and ruining her lawn. So although I really want to stay at my mom's house and be taken care of like the other children, I realize that I can't.

My brother watches the kids as Mom drives me the 35 miles back to my empty house. I hobble into the kitchen and make myself some hot tea, swallow some Tylenol and decide to spend the rest of the evening on the couch with my foot propped up. It hurts and my head hurts.

Husband eventually comes home, glances at my foot and asks me, "Why did you step on that rake?"

FAULT LINE: HOLE IN MY HEAD

We're landscaping around the perimeter of a new house, in a new state. This is a coastal state, so the soil is a mixture of sand and dirt which doesn't grow certain plants very well. The previous tenants had neglected the yard, so I decide one weekend to pull out the dead, dying, and bedraggled growth, and clean things up.

Husband is puttering around in my general vicinity, cleaning drains, gutters, and lopping off big tree branches. I am on my hands and knees, edging along sideways as I work. My knees are stiff, my back hurts, and after a few hours of this, I have to stand up and stretch.

So I push myself up from the ground, and *WHACK* the top of my skull against the bottom of an air conditioning unit that I didn't realize I was kneeling under. My skull has rammed into the sharp metal corner with enough force to puncture through the scalp, and this really hurts like hell.

I fall back down on my aching knees, swearing a lot, holding my head and feeling pissed off that I hadn't looked up, before I stood up.

Husband comes over as I kneel cursing in the dirt and sand, and checks the bleeding hole in my head. He asks me, "What did you stand up under the air conditioner for?"

FAULT LINE: I'M NOT HELPING YOU ANYMORE

We've purchased a new headboard for one of the kid's beds. Husband has attached it to the metal frame of the bed, and now it's time to re-assemble everything. We lift the box spring together, guiding it onto the metal side rails. It doesn't quite fit, so I kneel by the side of it and use my hand to push the slight overhang of the box spring in, and then push it down.

Unknown to me, Husband has also pushed his side of the box spring down, not knowing that my hand was there on the opposite side. The result is, my thumb somehow gets caught tightly between the box spring and the metal side rail and it does not yank loose.

This hurts like holy *hell*. It hurts so badly, that I am literally speechless with pain… my body is rigid, mouth open in an O, eyes popped wide. I'm not even breathing. Husband stands there and looks at me.

"What's wrong? What's the matter? Honey? Why aren't you answering me? What happened? Why aren't you talking?"

All I can do is gesture with my free hand towards my entrapped thumb, which feels as though it's being squashed flat in a giant vise.

As he comes over to where I am, my lungs suddenly expand and I yell, loudly—

"OOOOWWWOWOWOWOW!!!!!!!!!!!"

I'm pretty sure it was something similar to that.

He lifts the box spring, which causes even *more* pain, if such a thing is possible, and mercifully, my thumb is free. It feels like it's on fire, its throbbing like mad and I sit there and hold it in my other hand and rock back and forth and cry and yell, "OWWTHIS FUCKING HURTSOWOWOW!"

Husband pulls my hand towards him and examines my thumb, even though I don't want any touching of my thumb, which *GODDAMN HURTS!*

He wiggles it experimentally from side to side, as I curse and punch him in the arm with my good hand, trying to make him let it go.

Finally, he pronounces it mashed and mangled, but unbroken. He brings me crushed ice in a plastic baggie and makes me wrap it around to keep the swelling down. I sit there on the floor, snuffling, my thumb aching like fury, even though it's becoming half-frozen, and feeling absolutely sorry for myself.

He lifts the mattress onto the box spring and pushes the bed over to the wall. He then looks down at me and asks, "Why did you put your thumb in there like that?"

FAULT LINES: HEAD BANGER

We're living in Louisiana in a rental house. It's not a large house and doesn't have a garage, but there is an attached carport. On the back wall of the carport is an old work table. This is covered with all sorts of the boys projects, which are mostly old appliances they collect, then break down for the motors and parts, then reassemble the pieces into something or other.

I don't really care what they're building, as long as they are busy and out of my hair for part of the day.

I'm in the kitchen, loading the dishwasher, when the back door opens and I hear both of them calling for me. I turn to see Kyle, he's holding a hand over his forehead. Kevin is standing beside him saying, "Mom, I think you gotta take him to the 'mergency room."

"What's the matter?" I ask.

"He hit his head," Kevin says.

"Aw, honey," I say, drying my hands off with a dish towel and walking over to his brother, "Are you hurt?"

"I'm hurt a little," Kyle says, and as he lifts his hand, a large squarish piece of skin falls down to his eyes and blood begins to seep down his face.

"*OHMIGOD!*" I shriek in horror and disbelief, as Kyle leans forward a little, then calmly flips his forehead back up with his hand and holds it in place once more. He lifts a corner of his shirt up to swipe at the blood in his eyes.

"*How in God's name did you DO that!*" I cry out, grabbing a clean dish towel and pressing it to his head.

He said he had dropped something on the garage floor. He bent to retrieve it, and when he stood back up, had hit his head on the underside of the old work table, which had a sharp edge.

It slid right under the entire flap of forehead skin like a cheese slicer.

Adrenalin had shot through me and now I had the shakes, I'm trembling and trying to see how badly he is hurt. His forehead is exposed from the hairline down, as though someone had sliced through the top layer of skin and just peeled it down. No bone is showing or anything, and his hairline should hide any scar, but his head needs to be seen by a doctor, for sure.

I call Husband on the phone, grab more clean towels and we all head over to the hospital. Husband has said he'll meet me there in ten minutes, which is always such a lie, because he has no concept of time whatsoever.

In the emergency room, a doctor points a little flashlight at my sons pupils, which do what they're supposed to do, and the doctor announces he'll live. A nurse cleans all the blood off his face and neck, and a doctor spackles and glues the flap of skin back where it's supposed to be. They pad it all up with bandages and wind about half of a mile of white gauze around the top of his head. He looks like a miniature war victim.

After all the fun is over, Husband steps off an elevator, glances at the little gauze turban on Kyle's head and asks me what happened. I tell him and he looks at me and says, "What in the world did you let him hit his head like that for?"

FAULT LINES: BEAMED

We're living in Louisiana, in a huge white concrete house on the bayou. It has a two car garage attached to a huge boat storage/garage bay, with an enclosed workshop in the back. Husband has scrap and project wood stacked all over in the boat garage, since he has no boat.

Sheets of plywood, fencing, beams. Lots of tall, heavy wooden beams. The boat garage has openings in the outer wall, so the air can flow through and help keep the mold down.

I'm standing in the boat garage, trying to talk to him about something or other, as a storm is brewing outside. The wind is picking up; leaves are whirling around and suddenly, as is common on the Gulf, the storm hits. Water is pouring down and the wind is pushing it into the open bay of the boat garage, soaking the wood. Husband starts to move all the wood to the back of the building as I am calling out to him, *"Come in out of this storm!"*

Lightning is flashing, thunder is rumbling, and the wind is so loud, it's hard to speak or hear anything over the noise. I stand in the back of the building so the rain doesn't soak me, as he lines the heavy wooden beams along the wall, upright. I yell over the howling wind, *"Those beams will blow over standing up like that! Just lie them down on the floor!"*

Husband shakes his head to indicate nonsense, they won't fall over, and keeps standing the heavy beams upright against the wall. I turn to go inside the house, where sensible people should be during such a storm, but as I reach the door to the workshop, a wind of *tremendous* force whips into the boat garage. It pins the door shut as I try to force it open, and as I turn to call for help, a sharp, sickening pain explodes inside my head and I fall against the door.

I'm trying to see, but I can't focus. The pain is so bad, my hands are holding my head together, and I know if I let go, surely my head will just crack into pieces and fall to the ground.

I hear Husband shout my name and find myself sitting on the floor. He lifts a heavy beam off me and crouches down, pulling on my wrists...but I hold tight to my head, so it doesn't fall off. "Stop," I manage to say, "Stop pulling at me."

"Let go," he says, "So that I can see your head. Honey, let *go.*"

I let go of my throbbing head and immediately feel a rush of hot wetness run over my forehead and down onto my face. The pain is incredible and I am dizzy with it. Husband takes the edge of his shirt and wipes the blood away and peers at my head.

"How bad is it," I manage to ask, "Do I need stitches?"

"No," he says, "You've got a good gash and there's an egg-sized bruise already, but it doesn't need to be stitched. You're okay."

He pulls me to my feet and I try to stand steadily, but it hurts so badly, I just weave back and forth, one hand braced against the workshop door for support. Husband looks at me and says, "Why didn't you get out of the way when that beam fell over?"

FAULT LINES: BAD DOG

I'm working on our mini-farm in the Northeast, doing some chores and cleaning up the yard in general. Husbands obnoxious unneutered Newfoundland is running around in his huge exercise pen, which is surrounded by an eight foot chain link fence. It is positioned in back of the barn, with a large dog door cut through one wall, so he can access his indoor pen.

He is in the pen because every time this dog gets near me, he grabs my thigh in his jaws and proceeds to drag me around the yard, as if I were nothing more than a giant chew toy. He doesn't bite, but he does hold me and I can't get loose, no matter how many times I pound on his massive head with my fist.

As I work near the barn, he periodically makes a run at the outer gate, hitting it at full force with his entire body, trying to force it open. It shakes, but stays closed. Now and then I yell at him to "*STOP IT!*" He grins a doggy grin and ignores me.

I hate this dog.

I finally finish my work, walk over to the gate and stand looking at him. Normally, I don't feed or water this animal, Husband handles it when he gets home, but we're going away for the weekend and I want all the chores completed, so we can be on our way when he finishes work.

There is no water spigot near this pen, just a spigot on the side of the house, but the house is waaay over there, and the hoses aren't long enough to reach the pen. A set of longer hoses are on my shopping list for Lowes, but that isn't going to solve my problem today.

I wave my hands at the dog. "Get back," I say. "*SIT DOWN.*" He looks at me and after a few seconds, obligingly sits down on his broad, furry butt. I plan to open the gate the tiniest bit, just enough to grab the water bucket and slam the gate shut.

He watches me. I don't trust him.

I hold the gate tightly with one hand, and with the other, lift the latch. My body is poised to move quickly, grab the bucket and pull it out...but as soon as the latch is free of the metal pole, the Newf springs up on his hind legs and *pounces* against the gate with his front paws, like someone smacking a volleyball back across a net. The sturdy metal gate smashes right into my face, and as I cry out in pain and stagger backwards, the dog forces his way through the open gate and takes off, running.

My hands are on my face, I am bent forward, taking little breaths and trying to recover. My tongue gingerly touches my teeth, one by one, and encounters a jagged edge...tongue then fishes around and finds something, and I spit nearly a third of a tooth onto my palm.

The dog has run down the long driveway, across the country road and disappeared into the field across from our property. I hope the damned thing never comes back.

I get into my truck and drive straight to the dentist, praying he will be in his office, and he is. I hand him the chipped remnant, but he can't fix it, so he molds me a new tip for the broken tooth, which he says should last awhile until it needs a cap. Unless the force of the blow kills the tooth root of course, and then I'll need a root canal, he says.

Wonderful. Now I *really* hate this fucking dog.

I drive from the dentist over to Husbands office, show him the repaired tooth and the bruise forming on my face. He says, "Why did you let the dog knock the gate open and get out like that?"

FAULT LINES: ONE SMALL STEP

The kids are at my parents house. It's summer time, and the grass is thick and green. My only daughter, Lori, is running around the back yard, barefoot, when suddenly she cries out and falls to the ground. She draws her leg up and holds the ankle, crying. I run over to see what has happened, and she says she hurt her ankle by stepping in some hole.

I don't see a hole anywhere, but I get on my hands and knees to pat the lawn, and find a deep depression in the grass, where the earth has sunken down and the thick green grass has grown, filling it in, making it appear level and sound. Unknowingly, she stepped into this hole as she ran, twisting her ankle badly. It's swollen and she can't put her weight on it.

A trip to the emergency room shows no broken bones, but after some painful (but necessary) poking, prodding and pulling, the doctor states that she has probably torn some muscle and/or ligaments, and her lower leg should be casted.

I call Husband to tell him, and he instructs me to let the emergency room doctor do this, as he is working and cannot come to this emergency room to cast it himself.

He gets home late at night, glances at the cast and declares he could have applied a much nicer one. He says to me, "Why did you let her step in that hole?"

FAULT LINES: UNEXPECTED CONTENTS

We are moving in a few months and I am cleaning out the garage with Kevin's help. It's a mess and cluttered to the hilt, because Husband is a packrat and hardly ever throws anything away, for fear he will "need it someday."

We make a point of working on this mess only on the days Husband is at the office, so that there is not an endless series of arguments between he and I over Things I Wish To Throw Away Or Donate (like 99% of the stuff in the garage) and Things Husband Thinks Should Be Saved Forever (which is 100% of the junk in the garage).

We empty shelves, boxes, bins and sort it out into piles designated as Utter Trash, Give Away and We'll Let Him Keep This For a While.

Give Away means it is destined for our local Goodwill store, and we load the back of my Expedition at least once a day and make a run to deposit stuff in the big donation bin outside their main doors. Husband calls during the day to see what I am up to, and sometimes I say, "Oh, just cleaning out a little, you know. Kevin found another box of his old video game systems and we're donating that. When are you coming home?"

I always check to see when he is going to be done at the hospital and head home, so that Kevin and I can coordinate our secret runs to the dumpster and the Goodwill without his knowledge. Husbands main concern are the donation receipts. "Make *sure* you get a receipt for whatever you donate. And have them itemize everything, so I can take it off my taxes."

"But they don't itemize anything," I say to him, "They're volunteers, they just sign a receipt and hand it to me. We can't possibly itemize everything, it would take all day."

His tone turns slightly suspicious. "How could it take all day? What are you taking over there, anyway?"

Kevin nudges me and I say hastily, "I only meant that Goodwill Industries runs on volunteers at times, and sometimes people who work there are a little... um... mentally challenged. They can't really stand there and list each item, David."

"I don't see why not."

"Last week, for instance. The receipt had a space at the top for Donor Name and Information, and when I told the guy we lived on Evergreen Lane, he got all confused and asked me how to spell Evergreen. I said you spell EVER and then you spell GREEN, and he still couldn't spell either one, poor soul. So I knew there was no way he would be able to produce an itemized list. If this guy couldn't spell 'ever' or 'green', it's likely he'd seize right up trying to spell 'used badminton racket' or '27 hangers of various sizes'. I didn't want to stress him."

"I cannot believe that you didn't get an itemized list. The IRS wants an *itemized list,*" he informed me.

"Well, you're not going to get one from this Goodwill store. I'll try to reconstruct what was in the bags we took over, and the IRS is going to have to live with that."

"Bags? You took *bags* of things to the Goodwill?"

"Um... a few. Small bags. Old... socks and... and... (*"old sneakers,"* Kevin whispers) old sneakers and a few of my old handbags."

"Just as long as it wasn't bags of *my* stuff."

"No, no, no, we're packing all *that,*" I lied, gesturing at Kevin to for heaven's sake tie up that last big Hefty garbage bag full of Husbands garage junk. "So listen, are you coming home soon?"

I point to the Expedition and Kevin hefts the heavy bag into the back, and then closes the tailgate.

"Maybe in an hour, there's an ankle fracture I have to see in the ER first."

"Okay... see you then." I snap my cellphone shut and shove it into the front pocket of my jeans. "We have one hour to get rid of this stuff," I say, as we climb hastily into the car and start down the driveway. We drive to the Goodwill store and once again, encounter the same guy we had met on the previous trip, who couldn't spell Evergreen.

"More stuff, huh?" he asks, as Kevin opens the tailgate and starts to unload the five big bags of Give Away items that are stashed in the back.

"Yes, more stuff. Listen, is there anyone in the office that can give me a receipt that lists some of the items I'm donating? At least the number of boxes or bags that we drop off?"

"Well, I'm the only one here doin' receipts today. What all does it need to say?"

"You can just write down miscellaneous household goods, and list the number of bags, please."

"Okay," he says, as Kevin sets the last bag by the donation box and shuts the tailgate. The man scribbles on a donation receipt and hands it to me. I tell him thanks for the help, stuff the paper in my purse and start for home.

Husband gets home later in the evening and asks for the receipt. I retrieve it from my purse and hand it to him.

"It was the same guy who couldn't spell Evergreen," I explain, as he squints at the scribbled handwriting on the paper, "But at least he wrote down the number of bags, and I told him to just write down miscellaneous for the contents."

He holds the receipt back out to me and I take it, reading it for the first time. I start to giggle, then show it to Kevin, who grins, widely. We both start laughing, because it's truly so funny.

In crude letters under "Donation Items", the man at the Goodwill had helpfully scribbled these words: "*8 bags of mice*"

Husband looks at me and says, "Why did you let him misspell miscellaneous?"

FAULT LINES: GRACEFUL

We're in the process of moving from the Deep South back up to the Northeast. As usual, I have done all the packing of our household goods and personal belongings for the long trip to our new home. Our great room in this house is enormous, at least 30 by 40 feet. I decide to use the entire back half of it to store the boxes that are ready to go on the moving van, which is arriving in about five days. I've been at this for weeks and I'm worn out.

Our daughter, Lori, is staying in the South. She is packing her things and getting ready for a move to her own apartment, but she's still working all day. This means that I get stuck babysitting her two small dogs, neither of which is house trained. They run under my feet *constantly* as I work at packing and hauling boxes.

After nearly falling over them at least a dozen times, I buy a wire dog enclosure, a sort of portable play area. The panels are about 30 inches tall, and I set this up by the mountain of cardboard boxes in the great room. I line the floor with newspapers, put in bowls of water and food, toys, their cushiony bed, and incarcerate the little beasts while I work.

They don't like this doggie playpen and leap continually at the sides, yap incessantly and in general, drive me nuts, like Husband is doing now.

He does not pack so much as a shoebox, claiming he is busy with work and phone calls, and while it may have taken *me* weeks to pack *my* stuff, *his* stuff will only take two or three hours, tops.

Whatever, I say to him, and continue to pack his books, his knife collection, his fishing gear, his clothes, his collectibles and generally continue to exhaust myself as the moving day gets closer.

One morning, I am too tired to even get showered or dressed. I schlump around in pajamas, an old long robe, big fuzzy slippers, and try to wake up. The dogs have peed gallons on the newspapers and are leaping and yapping in their pen for their breakfast. Even though Husband has been up for hours, he is on his cell phone, ignoring the dogs and the noise.

I grab a black plastic trash bag and mutter loudly about how *some* people could have let me *sleep* this morning by feeding these freaking *dogs* and they could have picked up the damned smelly *newspapers,* and he waves a hand at me to indicate that he can't hear whoever is on the phone and ignores me.

I lean over the pen, trying to roll up the wet papers, but the dogs are leaping in the urine and yapping. So, I gather my robe up in one hand and swing my leg over the pen, but my fuzzy slipper catches on the top rail and won't come loose. My entire body is still in a forward momentum, however, and this causes me to topple right over the pen and *crash* onto the slate floor, landing hard on my right side.

My fuzzy slipper is still caught on the top wire, and this has pulled the whole dog pen over on top of me as well.

I have landed squarely in the urine, knocked over the bowl of water, and the dogs are dancing all about and over me and on top of me and yapping.

Husband has not missed a beat in his conversation, other than to say, "Honey, what are you *doing*?"

He dashes over to where I lie stunned on the floor in a large puddle of dog pee, and with *no pause in conversation,* he lifts the entangled dog pen off of me with one hand, while holding his cell phone with the other and saying into it, "Oh, it's nothing, my wife just fell."

Aftershock pain floods my body, especially my right leg, which took the brunt of the fall…I'm fearful I may have broken a bone. I manage to sit up and pain ricochets down my leg, centering in the middle of my right shin, which hurts so badly I can't even touch it.

Husband is *still* talking on his cell phone as he extends a hand to help me up off the floor. He looks surprised when I smack it away.

I decide that I am going to start crying, loudly, because I deserve to. So I turn over and start to crawl off the wet newspapers and the detritus underneath me, crying and dragging my hurt leg behind me, like in a scene from a bad movie.

He says to the phone, "Look, I have to go, call me later."

I drag myself down the hall, crying the entire time as he follows me, talking nonstop.

"Want me to help you up? Where does it hurt the most? Why are you crying? Did you hear a crack? Why didn't you take my hand? Are you mad? Are you just hurt? Is that why you're crying? Want me to look at your leg? Think you can stand up? Why aren't you answering me?"

I drag myself to the laundry room and pull clean sweatpants and a t-shirt out of the dryer.

I sit on my ass on the cold slate floor and get dressed, crying the entire time. He's on his knees now, trying to probe the bones in my shin and I yell that I will let any other doctor on the entire *planet* look at my leg, *except him!*

He is totally confused over this, which is normal for him, and I drag myself out the back door, down the deck stairs and over to his truck, where I have to tolerate him lifting me up under the arms to get me on the seat.

Once in the emergency room, I am x-rayed and examined by a doctor, who wisely does not comment when I angrily refuse a consultation from the doctor who drove me here, as he says, "Well... uh... I'll have... someone... take a look at these films a little later, then."

I am put in a cast from knee to foot for a possible hairline fracture of my tibia and fibula, and am then driven back home.

I have stopped crying and hobble into the house on crutches and collapse on the couch.

Husband stands there, looking down at me and says, "*Now* would you like to tell me why you went and fell over that dog pen this morning?"

CONSTRUCTION DAZE

We have owned many houses over the course of our marriage, done many renovations, and had many adventures along the way. Here are a few minor episodes from our construction daze...er, days.

A HOLE IN ONE

The very first house we ever bought was an old, old Colonial/something. It had three stories and a huge front porch and sat on a skinny lot, in a neighborhood full of houses on skinny lots, most of them sharing one driveway. There were original gas lines in the walls, knob and tube wiring, and wallpaper on the ceilings... we're talking *old*. But it had wonderfully high ceilings, arched doorways, it felt like home, and that's what always counts, right?

I unpacked boxes, arranged furniture, and started to settle in. There was an odd little corner wall in the front hallway that faced the front door, and I decided to hang a mirror on it one afternoon. But it wouldn't hold a nail, no matter where I placed it. Tapping on the wall only led to a hollow sound.

Husband came home and I told him about it. He tapped on the wall, up and down, left and right. "I don't think there's a stud behind it," he announced.

"Strange," I said, running my hand up and down over the old wallpaper. "It's such a funny place for a piece of wall." Then I thought of the built in cabinets in the corners of the dining room. "Maybe it's a cabinet and the previous owner just walled it off. I'll have to ask the lady next door if she knows anything about it. It would be interesting to know, don't you think?"

Husband picks up the hammer I had been using, then suddenly swings it back and *crashes* it through the wall a few times as dust flies all around and I stand there with my mouth open. Sure enough, behind the jagged holes gouged in the wall, you could see the original, unused shelves still in place. I wave a hand back and forth in front of my face, trying to clear the dust.

"Why did you *do* that?" I ask, looking at him in bewilderment.

"What? You said you wanted to know what was behind there," he answers, handing me the hammer.

"I didn't expect you to smash it with a hammer! I was going to ask the neighbor! *Look at all those holes!*" I gesture at the wounded wall and shake my head, frowning.

"Oh, I can fix that," he says, taking the hammer back from me. He then knocks down the rest of the entire wall, *CRASHBLAMWHACK,* as I stand there in amazement, too shocked and surprised to even yell at him, which is rare for me.

He kisses me on top of my head and hands me the hammer. "There you go," he says, "Now there are no more holes."

ALL FALL DOWN

Our first home must at one point have been a boarding house, I reasoned, based on the layout of the upstairs rooms, which were all in a sort of circle surrounding a central hall, with only one bathroom at the end.

Since it was impossible to take the ancient wallpaper off in the bedrooms without destroying the plaster, I decided to just paint over it. This actually worked pretty well, with only minor bubbling here and there, so I was pleased.

The smallest bedroom was painted last. It was also the only room in the house with wallpaper on the ceiling... hmm. I walked around the room, staring up... got on a ladder and peeled at a corner... the paper stuck tight. Why had only this ceiling been papered? Had there been damage of some sort, and possibly the previous owners had covered it up?

I said to Husband, "Maybe we should get someone to look at it, this is a really old house. We don't know what's under there."

"No," he said, "What for? We'll just paint it like we did the walls, it will be fine, trust me."

So he climbed up on a ladder to paint the ceiling. As he finished a few last spots, I cleaned the area up, gathering paint cans and brushes. I had just gotten to the bottom of the stairs with it all, when I heard this weird sort of cracking rumbly noise and then a loud *CRASH.*

A big cloud of white dusty stuff was billowing out into the upstairs hall as I ran back up the stairs, yelling, *"DEAR GOD WHAT WAS THAT??!!"*

Husband was still standing on the ladder when I ran in through the doorway, coughing and trying to locate him in the dust filled room. He was covered in white powdery stuff and pieces of plaster. Apparently the only thing holding the ceiling up had been the ancient wallpaper.

When it got wet from the paint, the entire thing just gave way and crashed to the floor, all except for the small square which was directly over his head. He climbed down and looked at the mess on the floor... looked up at the tiny patch of ceiling that was left... then looked at me and said, "I think I'm done painting ceilings for the day, okay?"

WOUNDED KNEE

One of the first houses we owned in the Northeast was a wonderful, old three story Victorian. It had one major flaw: a tiny, outmoded kitchen. Not only was it tiny, it was *waaay* in the back of this huge house, as had been the style when originally built, back in the early 1900's. Husband had promised he would build me a new kitchen when we sold our previous house and got settled financially, so when both of these things happened, I happily called construction people and started getting estimates.

Kitchens are *expensive*, they can cost anywhere from a Lincoln Town Car to a Porsche, depending on how roomy or elaborate you wish to get. They are about Minivan price if you do the interior work yourself, so after a lot of arguing and price comparison, we decided to build a Minivan kitchen. We picked a contractor who said he could start having the foundations dug in about two weeks.

The sight of sweaty, muscled men in work crews armed with shovels and excavating equipment can do things to a woman... oh, get your mind out of the gutter, not in *that* way. But you stand there and watch them dig and think to yourself, *well, as long as they're here with all these tools and everything, maybe I should have them just, you know, dig out a space for a new family room, too... and maybe a new back entrance, since the old one is so small... and a sort of mudroom off of that...*

Then the guys with the cement truck roll in and you're really in trouble... *and maybe a small walkway along the back of the house, where it's always such a mess... and maybe a path to the garden... and a little cement pad under the hose where it's always so muddy... ohhh, and maybe a sweet little patio off the back of the new family room, so I can sit out at night, have a cup of tea....*

And you point here and gesture over there and sketch little pictures on the sides of wooden boards and before you know it the work crews are constructing a Rolls Royce and a Lamborghini in your back yard.

Bills get higher and higher and your eyes open wider and wider, and once the walls are up, the roof on, and wiring and plumbing are installed, you are forced to put a halt to the luxury sports car kitchen, and wave goodbye to the construction crews. You look at the expensive shell of this addition and realize you can't drive it anywhere because while it may have a roof, four wheels and some doors, it doesn't have seats, a steering column, or an engine.

This means you go to the Lowes Home Improvement Store, open an account and basically sign away your soul to their credit department so that you can buy new appliances and kitchen cabinets. Kitchen cabinets cost a lot of money if you have a professional install them, so Husband decided that we would install our own.

I wasn't keen on this idea for several reasons. First, those danged things are *heavy* to lift out of the bed of a pick-up truck, and I knew that my kids would disappear as soon as the truck rumbled up and I hollered for them to come and help. Second, I knew that no matter where I asked for the cabinets to be placed, Husband would argue with me about their arrangement. Third, he never remembers that I am much smaller and weaker than he is, and always assumes that I can simply dead lift a 60 pound wooden cabinet into the air over my head like he can and then hold it in place, while he fusses around with the drill before eventually securing the damned thing to the wall.

After much effort, arguing, and one outright fight, he finally managed to secure the base cabinets to the floor in the new kitchen roughly where I wanted them, but the new upper cabinets sat for *weeks* on my living room floor.

I was tired of walking around them and complained a lot, so Husband finally hauled them into the kitchen and started to work. He was using a little stepladder, and I was standing on top of the bottom cabinets, helping hold the heavy upper cabinet in place while he drilled holes and secured it to the wall.

Now, the bottom cabinets had no countertops yet... I was balancing my 110 pound body on top of the wooden edges of the bottom cabinets. This was a little tricky, but the cabinets were strong and I was not a large person, so I managed. When it came time to install those narrow cabinets that are on top of the fridge area, since Husband was only standing on a stepladder, he couldn't reach them with the drill.

"You have a taller ladder in the garage," I told him, "Go and get that, then you'll be able to reach."

"No, I'll just balance on the cabinets like you're doing," he says. "There's no need to bring in that ladder."

"Stand on the... are you out of your mind? Your feet are too big. You'll never be able to balance, you'll fall."

"My feet," he says, "are a completely normal size and I have *perfect* balance. I take karate, you know."

"Your feet," I reminded him, "are a size *sixteen,* there is no *way* you are going to be able to balance."

"Fine," he answers, "then I'll stand across the edges *and* the drawer part. That should give me enough support."

I raise an eyebrow and look him up and down. "There is no *way* that a one inch wooden support is going to hold your weight. You'll break the drawer."

"I am *not* going to break the drawer. You have no faith in me."

"You're right, I don't. Just go get the ladder."

He said he had trained for years in knowing exactly how much stress and strain and weight ratios and something or other human bones could take before they broke and if it applied to *bone,* it certainly applied to *wood.*

I said, "Well, Einstein, I don't care *what* you're trained in, only an *idiot* would deduce that a one inch strip of cheap wood will hold a 300 pound guy."

Which of course he ignored, so despite the fact I am yelling at him, *"Don't you dare stand on that!"* he stands on top of the flimsy drawer support and of course it snaps clean in half, and his foot crashes through the drawer bottom and down through the cabinet below, as the broken wood scrapes and cuts his leg all up.

I stand there totally pissed about the broken drawer and don't care about his bleeding leg as he disentangles himself from the cabinet. His knee is swollen to the size of a baseball and this he blames on *me,* in an attempt to make me feel guilty, but I don't feel guilty, not one bit.

Especially after I find out months later he had been kicked in that knee the *previous day* in karate, and hadn't wanted me to find out about it.

It just made me want to kick him in his injured knee a second time.

A TIGHT FIT

We owned a small farm once, with about eight acres of land in the Northeast. The house on this property was actually an old reconverted barn, but it wasn't anything like you would see in Architectural Digest, trust me. Everything was built (or had sagged) slightly off kilter and leaned either too far left or too far right, like the stairs to the second floor, which were definitely tilted.

This made quite a challenge for the moving guys when we first took up residence. They would start up the stairs carrying a dresser or something, and nearly halfway up start to stagger and have to shift the weight, as the tilt started to make maneuvers difficult.

Now, our master bedroom set was massive, and although I had lobbied hard to leave it in the big Victorian house, where it fit perfectly both in size and décor, Husband had insisted it come along with us while the major renovations were being done on that house. He couldn't sleep in any other bed, he declared.

The nightstands were bad enough at three feet long and 30 inches deep (not to mention that long ass dresser of his with the 4000 pound marble top), but the real killer was the headboard to the king sized bed frame. Constructed of solid wood, intricately carved, and with huge finials flanking a highly arched top piece, it was monstrously heavy and unwieldy to handle, let alone try to carry up a narrow set of tilting stairs on an old farm building.

It was also six feet tall, and when the moving guys (it took four of them, poor fellows) were finally able to lift it up the first three steps, they ran into an immediate problem. The top of the headboard scraped against a low-built bumper of some sort in the ceiling, directly over the initial steps. It wouldn't go up.

I called Husband who said it was nonsense, he was 6'3, and if *he* could make it up those steps, the headboard certainly could. I reminded him that he had to duck his head to go under the ceiling bumper thingie, and he said he had never done that, and I said oh yes he had, and that the headboard wasn't bendable and it wouldn't fit.

I said that I thought the moving guys ought to take it back to the big house where it belonged.

He said he was going to be home very soon, and that he would fix it, and that the bed was staying.

"How are you going to fix it?" I asked, "You can't stretch the ceiling, and you can't bend the wood."

"I am a surgeon," he replied, "I can fix *everything.*"

I made a face at the phone after we hung up and told the moving guys to just set the damned thing down in the living room for right now. They did, and then continued to unload the rest of the truck, as I started to slice through layers of sealing tape with a kitchen knife and began to unpack boxes.

I forgot about the headboard in the next few hours, because moving is chaotic, noisy and messy, and there was plenty of things to occupy my time and attention. Like the dead birds in the big red barn at the back of the property, which Chase discovered. He flung one out of the second story barn loft at Lori, who was standing down below on the grass, making her scream. This naturally caused him to fling a few more in her direction.

Husband pulled up in the driveway as I was yelling at Chase. He waved at me and then walked straight into the house carrying some longish metal box, as I smacked my middle son in the head, then ordered him to get a garbage bag and a shovel and clean up the damned birds or else.

Walking back into the house I suddenly heard a BUZZBUZZBUUUZZZZBUZZZZZZZZZZ and went running towards the noise, only to collide with the moving guys, who were all standing in a clump at the bottom of the stairs and staring open mouthed at Husband...who was standing there in a business suit, with plaster and dust falling all around him and onto his head, cutting noisily through the bumper thingie on the ceiling over the stairs with a Sawzall.

"What are you *doing*! DAVID!!! WHAT ARE YOU... DAAAVID!!!"

I held my hands over my ears and shouted, but he ignored me and kept sawing and sawing and sawing until a big, jagged edged semi-circle had been hacked through the ceiling piece that overhung the bottom of the stairs.

Debris littered the stairs and the floor and dust settled over all of us, as he finished and turned off the Sawzall, then stood back to take a better look. He unplugged the Sawzall from the wall and looked at me.

"Headboard should fit right up those stairs now," he said, coiling the cord around his hand and putting the Sawzall back inside its metal case. "I *told* you I could fix it. "

THE BIG BANG

Do you know what happens when you build a new kitchen, or a new anything? You get construction debris. Lots of it.

The big stuff is put into one of those portable dumpsters, but the cleanup crew rarely bothers themselves about the little stuff. The work guys wear heavy soled construction boots and crunch right over broken glass, nails and razor blades. Your kids trot happily after them in thin sandals or bare feet and eventually, these kids are ferried to the emergency room for a tetanus shot because they've stepped on or cut themselves on something rusty and old.

Kids also like loud power tools and seeing things knocked apart, or sawn apart, and messes created. Workmen sometimes let kids hold these power tools (until you catch them at it) and the kids learn all sorts of useful and harmful things as they run around after the these people, asking a jillion questions.

One afternoon I was painting in the new kitchen and heard the back door open. A few seconds later, I heard water running in the new utility room sink. "Who is that?" I call from my perch on the ladder.

"It's just us, Mommy," I hear my two youngest sons chorus, "We're getting a drink."

"Oh, okay, sweeties," I say, continuing to roll paint on the wall. The water stops, the door bangs, and I assume they go back outside. I work the roller up and down, up and down on the kitchen wall. About ten minutes later, I decide I need a break, and go to wash the paint off my hands in the utility room. But as I reach for the spigot, I notice the sink has wads of wet, bloody paper towels lying in the bottom of it. Naturally, I open the back door and yell, "*Boys!*"

Two blond heads poke around the corner of the new family room, blue eyes all wide and innocent. "Which one of you is *bleeding?*" I ask.

Both shrug and then their heads pop back out of sight. So I walk out into the debris strewn back yard and over to where they are, playing in a pile of scrap lumber the workmen have left behind. They have been busy hammering little wooden structures together, which would be fine, except for the fact there are small puddles of blood on the ground.

I point to the blood and say, "Okay, who got hurt? Tell Mommy right *now,* please, I won't be mad."

Kyle holds a hammer in both hands and looks at me, then at his brother. Kevin's hands are behind his back, so it's fairly easy to figure out who the injured party is here. "Let's see the damage," I say to him.

"Promise you won't make me get a shot," he says. I frown and walk right up to him, reaching for his hands, and he backs up a few steps. "Promise *first*", he says.

"I am not promising a *thing* young man, let me see your hands."

His chin lifts in a stubborn angle. "I'm *eight* now," he says, "I don't *have* to get a shot if I don't *want* one."

Kyle, ever the peacemaker says, "Don't worry, Mommy, he didn't use a *rusty* nail or anything, it was brand new."

Nail? I look at the hammers. "Did you drive a *nail* into your hand? Let me see it. *NOW!*"

Kevin's jaw juts out even farther. "You're just going to get *mad,"* he says, "I already put a Band-Aid on it, I'm not a *baby,* you know."

Kyle says, "Oh no, he didn't pound a nail in his hand or anything, he just sort of blew his finger up... but it's only one finger."

At this point, you just lunge at the damned kid, grab his wrists from behind him and force his hands to the front. You see his hand with the first finger dripping blood right through the Band-Aid, then you grab his wrist and haul him in the house after you, as he digs his heels in and shouts, *"I'm not getting a shot! I'm not getting a shot! I'm not getting a... HELP! HELP!"*

The dogs are barking and leaping around your feet as you wrestle him to the sink and stand behind him, mashing him into it so he can't get away. You peel off the blood soaked Band-aid to see his fingertip, actually exploded open in a neat hole and bleeding profusely, the skin all curled back in five little flaps, sort of like flower petals that have unfurled.

You turn on the water and using both your hands, grip his wrist and force his hand under the water while telling his brother to get you a clean towel, make sure it's *clean!* Kevin is screaming like a banshee more from anger than from anything else, and you yell at him, *"Just shut up! What the hell were you two doing?"*

Kyle explains over the din that the construction guys had left a lot of nails from the electric nail gun on the ground, and Kevin had thought it would be cool to see if they exploded like the work guys said they would if you hit one with a hammer. But even though he tried and tried to get it to explode, it didn't, no matter how many times he hit it.

"Uh huh," I say, still mashing Kevin against the sink and wrapping his hand up in the clean towel, "And neither one of you could figure out maybe something which *explodes* could have hurt you?"

I grab his wrist and hold it tight, and drag him after me to find my pocketbook, because I know if I let him go, he's just going to take off and run. Kyle trots after me as I drag his brother out the front door, who is insisting over and over he's *fine,* and if I make him get a shot he's gonna call the police and report me for *child abuse!*

"Go right ahead," I say, pulling him into the car and keeping my grip on him, "If they take me to jail, I can get some rest."

Since the hospital is only two blocks away, I hang onto my son as I drive to the emergency room. Kyle is still chattering. "See, he was hitting it and hitting it, so I said let *me* try, and I hit it and hit it and it still didn't explode, so we tried *another* one and *it* didn't explode, and I said this is stupid and that guy was probably fibbing about there being gunpowder on the top... "

I park the car and get out, pulling Kevin over the driver's seat with me. Kyle scrambles out, too, still talking.

"... and so then I said maybe if we hit just the gunpowder part it would work, but the hammer was too big, so we pounded the *first* nail inna block of wood, and then took *another* nail and held the tip of *that* one on the gun powder part, and Kevin hit it with the hammer and it *worked* this time."

I'm holding on with both hands to his brother, who is lunging from side to side, trying to escape and repeating,

"I am NOT getting a shot, I am NOT getting a shot, you can't MAKE me get a shot, I am NOT getting a shot!"

"Wonderful," I say, dragging Kevin over to the check-in window, "Your brother got the gunpowder to work and blew the top of his finger apart. He could have blown it *off.*"

But lecturing is useless at times like this, when you're standing in an emergency room with a bleeding, screaming kid, shouting over the noise that he's making for the clerk to please page his father and let him know we're here.

The emergency room doctor takes a preliminary look at the deep hole blasted in the bloody fingertip and announces it needs stitches. Kevin, who has been declaring endlessly that he is *not* getting a shot, now switches to, *"I am NOT getting stitches, I am NOT getting stitches, you can't MAKE me get stitches, I'll SUE!"*

I sit on the side of the stretcher and just keep a firm hold on his wrist, as we all wait for Dad. Kevin's brain is finally starting to process that he is going to need stitches and that he isn't going to get away from me, so now he starts to cry.

"You HATE me, you WANT to see me suffer, you WANT them to poke needles in my skin, I want my DAD, my DAD won't let them poke me, you WANT to see me suffer..."

A headache that promises to be a whopper is starting to form right behind my eyeballs.

Husband eventually wanders in from the depths of the hospital and says hey, buddy, to our wailing son, who shuts right up and then asks in a quivery voice, "Do I really need to have stitches, Daddy ?"

"Well, I think you're going to need a few," says Dad, "But you won't feel anything. We'll numb it up first with some magic medicine."

A nurse comes in with a big cotton ball soaked in green numbing stuff, and we hold it to the exploded fingertip until it goes numb. Dad folds the little flower petal skin flaps back down over the hole and everything is stitched neatly back into place, with me and three nurses helping to hold Kevin down, as Kyle pats his brothers leg and watches.

Ten days later the stitches need to come out and it's the same routine. *"You WANT me to suffer, you WANT me to be in pain, you WANT to stab me with tweezers!"*

He carries on so much that we have to wait until he is asleep, sneak to his bedside in the dark with a flashlight, and carefully *snipsnipsnip* the threads, in order to remove the damned stitches.

I make a vow to never have construction done again, ever, until Kevin is grown and has possibly moved to another planetary system.

STUPID THINGS
I'VE DONE #2

I ran out to the K-mart late one night. Threw a jacket on over my t-shirt, grabbed my pocketbook and out the door I went. Only needed bread and milk, so I was done in five minutes and standing in line with my cart. The lady standing behind me in line had glanced pointedly down at the floor quite a few times as I stood there, leafing through the tabloids, awaiting my turn.

I finally looked down to see what was so darned interesting on the floor, and realized that I had run out of the house wearing my daughter's big, orange, Garfield the Cat slippers. There is really no way to explain away this sort of thing. The solution is to stand there and act as though it's perfectly normal, and by all means, do *not* run or slink out the door before anyone else sees you. Stroll, like wearing bedroom slippers with giant furry cat heads on them in public is something that simply everybody should be doing.

During a busy holiday season, while walking in a crowded mall, I became separated from Husband amidst the throngs of shoppers. I tried and tried to reach him, repeatedly called his name, but to no avail. Lowering my head so that I could search for possible open spaces between the compacted bodies surrounding me, I finally snaked my way through the crowd, keeping my eye on his blue jacket in the distance.

When I finally reached him, I grabbed the back of his blue jacket and pulled on it sharply, saying, "Geezus *Christ*, didn't you hear me calling you?" Some tall, total stranger in a blue jacket turned around to stare stonily down at me. He had no holiday spirit.

While attempting to neaten up my eyebrows one evening with one of those Do-It-Yourself hot waxing kits, I didn't notice after I put the wax on and smoothed a paper strip over it, that the wax had oozed out on the side a little.

I waited until it cooled, yanked the paper strip off and when I inspected to see if it had removed the unwanted hairs, 3/4 of my right eyebrow was stuck on it. Take my advice and get your eyebrows done in a salon, otherwise, you look all fucked up for weeks until they grow back.

I was so tired one night that when I went to brush my teeth, I squeezed styling gel onto my toothbrush instead of toothpaste. It tastes disgusting, if this has never happened to you.

Conversely, I was once so mentally overwhelmed and distracted I squeezed toothpaste onto my hands, thinking it was styling gel. You can't get that shit out of your hair without major effort.

I was shopping with Husband once in a department store, and we were walking through the aisles, holding hands. I spied a fantastic outfit on a mannequin and let go of his hand to inspect the price tag, talking to him about how nice the style was, what a great color, I already had shoes to match, it would be perfect, etc.

With my eyes still glued on the outfit, which unfortunately was not on sale, I again took Husbands hand in mine and started to walk away, remarking that I'd have to make sure to ask a clerk if that outfit was going to be on sale anytime soon, because I am sure it would look great on me, didn't he agree? An unfamiliar voice answered back, saying that he agreed, the outfit would look great on me.

I stopped in my tracks and turned my head to see a total stranger standing next to me, our fingers securely interlaced. He smiled down at me and I know my mouth fell open. I pulled my hand away and backed up, looking for Husband, who instead of staying by my side, had wandered away to look at a display of men's ties. I hadn't noticed, had reached for him and instead found myself holding hands with the man whose girlfriend had also stopped by the mannequin to admire the outfit. Her boyfriend thought it was funny. She didn't seem to possess quite the same sense of humor about it.

Husband bought me the outfit in compensation for my trauma.

I was grocery shopping one day and being driven crazy by my two youngest sons, who were in the habit of throwing all sorts of items they wanted into the cart that I did not wish to purchase. I had parked the cart and wandered down the aisle a little ways... forgot exactly what it was I was trying to find, but anyway, a short time later I came back to the cart and sure enough, there was a ton of things I didn't recognize in the basket. I started yanking them out and stuffing them on the nearest shelf in a jumble, and said, *"You damned kids better stop throwing this extra shit in my cart, do you hear me?"*

Some lady walked up to me and stared at the cart, then at the items on the shelf, then at me. It was her cart, and her groceries I had just tossed out onto the shelf. While I had been searching for whatever-it-was, the boys had pushed my shopping cart over into the next aisle and I hadn't noticed.

If this ever happens to you, just apologize profusely and very carefully put everything precisely back into the cart, and remind yourself that strangling children is against the law.

BOOK JACKET
DILEMMAS

zeecee: Hallie! Halllieee! Please be here please be here

Halliegirl: Alright, already, I'm here. What's the panic?

zeecee: Took you long enough! I have a new blurb thingie for you to read

Halliegirl: Is it *vastly* different than the previous offering?

zeecee: Different as can be, you'll see:

The author of this work remains a mystery. All we know is that the manuscript was delivered by pelican. Once it was retrieved from the gullet, we shook out a few dead fish, hung the pages up to dry and read it. It wasn't too sucky, so since the boss was gone and we had nothing else better to do that week, we ran off a few thousand copies and decided to hand them out for free. Enjoy.

zeecee: Well?

zeecee: Well???

zeecee: Hallie? Are you on the phone or something? Or so struck with wonder at what you've read, you're speechless? Hal??? SPEAK to me...

Halliegirl: Oh, I think it safe to say I am struck dumb alright. Are you, or were you HIGH when you wrote this?

zeecee: ~GASP~ High? I'm possibly the most boringly straight person you'll ever meet in your life! High?! ME?! No, I wasn't *high*...

Halliegirl: Zee. I love you, you know this. But that reads as though you were stuck on some desert island like some crazy sun fried hermit writing on palm tree bark or something. Then you communed with Brother Pelican to take Your Words to the World, and he flew them to a group of loony workers who took advantage of their absent boss by basically declaring anarchy and distributing them for free to the masses.

zeecee: Wow, did you even take a breath while typing all that?

Halliegirl: I took a lot of breaths as I was reading what you sent. Zee! Pelicans, gullets, and dead fish?????????

zeecee: Doesn't have quite the same ring as lions and tigers and bears, oh my, huh...

Halliegirl: No.

zeecee: Well, I was a little tired when I wrote it... okay, I was a lot tired, plus, I was huddled in a blanket late at night at my desk, writing, feeling a bit hermitish perhaps... staring at the soft glow of the computer screen... the room in utter darkness except for that luminescence...

Halliegirl: Haagen Daz bar clutched firmly in your grasp as you sat mesmerized by the glow.

zeecee: Kinda sorta... hey, maybe you and I should write something together...

Halliegirl: It would all come out looking exactly like this conversation, Zee. Okay, here's my thoughts on pelicans and dead fish. NO.

zeecee: Sigh, sigh, sigh... fine... I will go back to the drawing board and task my brain AGAIN...

Halliegirl: Set that brain of yours to *NORMAL,* just once. Pretty please.

zeecee: ~trudges away, grumbling... ~

HUSBAND
(HOMOSAPIEN
ECCENTRICUS)

NEAR DEATH IN THE SAM'S CLUB

We are living in one of the mid-Atlantic states. Our new home is a nice one, but it does need some updating and minor repair in a few places.

Nearly every weekend, Husband and I make the 20 minute drive down the highway to the next larger town that has everything in it that our small town doesn't. At some point, this highway snakes through the middle of one of those retail sections, where the big chain stores are all in a row, on both sides. Target, Old Navy, Lowe's, Toys R Us, Office Depot…you name it, that section of the highway has it.

We make a master plan as we approach this section. Do we go to the Walmart and Sam's Club first, then cross the intersection and hit Target, then Bed, Bath and Beyond? Or do we drive down a little farther to the next traffic light, so we can hit Toys R Us *before* we get to the Target? Do we stop at Wendy's for a bite to eat before or after we go to Pet Smart and Borders?

Decisions, decisions, and it almost always causes a fight (or a near fight) between the two of us, or at the very least, a strongly worded discourse. I mean, I have been with Husband for over 25 years and would give him the last drop of my blood if he needed it, but the man drives me to the brink of insanity at times.

Writing about the brinks could make an entire book in itself, and one of these days I might do that. Then if he ever makes a comment on how tired I look, I can thrust the book at him and say, "Here's part of the reason *why*, sweetheart."

So we are on one of these weekend trips, arguing about where to shop first, and this weekend Sam's Club is not on the list. We simply do not need to go there. There are no king-sized food items we need to buy, and we still have ten pounds of frozen burritos leftover in the extra freezer in the garage from the last time.

I don't react as the Sam's Club sign looms into view. Husband adores Sam's Club and would shop there every day if he could so naturally he asks me, "Do you want to go to Sam's Club?"

"No."

"Okay. Where's the first place we're going, again?"

"Lowes, I need paint for the bathroom and we need to check the prices on molding."

"Sam's Club is coming up before we get to Lowe's. Sure you don't want to stop on the way?"

"No. We need to go to Lowe's. Every time we go to Sam's, we're there for three hours and you come out with about 400 pounds of frozen food that barely fits in the freezers. There is nothing we need in the Sam's Club, I told you this before we left."

"You're being silly, honey, we don't buy 400 pounds of frozen food. But it's fine, if you don't want to go to Sam's, we won't go."

We stop at a red light and I check to make sure that I've brought the paint sample with me for the paint guy. Mentally, I mull over anything else that I might need from the Lowe's. The traffic light turns green. Husband shifts slightly in his seat and accelerates the truck, slowly.

"You're *sure* you don't want to stop in Sam's? I mean, it's right here, we can turn in right here."

"No! For like the fourth time, we don't need to go to Sam's."

"I didn't ask you four times. Look, here's the entrance."

"Drive by it! Which part aren't you hearing? We don't need to go!"

"I can't concentrate on driving if you yell. You don't have to yell, I can hear you."

"Then quit repeating yourself and making me raise my voice. I-do-not-want-to-go-to-Sam's."

He turns the truck into the Sam's Club entrance and zips into an empty parking spot. It is moments like these that just make your face go all wrong. Your eyes squeeze shut, your nostrils expand, and your mouth screws up in some sort of shape it shouldn't be in, and you feel your insides start to tighten.

"*Why* did you turn into Sam's Club, when I *just said*, we didn't need to *go there?*"

"You were yelling. I can't concentrate when you're yelling at me, so I turned in here."

He switches off the ignition and turns his head to look at me. I stare steadily at him in return.

"I wasn't yelling, but I *could*. I was enunciating the words. Turn the truck back on and drive back out and take me to Lowe's, please."

I tap the paint sample on the dashboard, firmly, and point it in the direction of Lowe's, to show him I mean business.

"Honey, we're here already. Let's just stop in for a minute." He rolls out of the truck before I can say another word.

I roll down the window to call after him, testily, "I am *not* going to come in there! Get back in this truck and take me to Lowe's!"

"Okay," he calls back as I see him take out his wallet to obviously search for his Sam's card, "I'm out of vitamins, so I won't be long, maybe ten minutes."

This pronouncement causes me to spend at least two minutes cursing loudly in the confines of the truck, punching the upholstery repeatedly with my fist. Then I throw myself out of the door, sling my pocketbook over my shoulder, slam the door, muttering and cursing as I do, and walk fast-n-mad after him. I know that if I don't go after him that I'll be sitting in the truck until the damned store closes.

I snap out my blue plastic Sam's card to the lady at the door who doesn't even look at it, grab a cart to hold my pocketbook (it's heavy, so what), and march it fast in the direction that I last saw him.

He's up there to the right in the television and computer aisles already. Vitamins are displayed clear over to the extreme left of the store, past the 57 checkout stands. I open my pocketbook to stuff the Sam's card back into the wallet, lift my head up to see where he is and he is…gone.

He's not in the television aisles anymore.

I trundle the cart over there in case he is bending over, examining something electronic on a lower shelf, perhaps. He's not there. Next, I stand on tiptoe and scan the closest areas for his head and shoulders. At 6'3" he's pretty easy to spot in stores, even at a distance.

There, his head is down next to the appliances lined up on that far wall. How did he get down there so fast? I start wheeling the cart in and around people and displays and then aim it in the direction of his head. Which then disappears around the corner… *sigh*

I get waylaid by a huge pallet of dog food being ferried down the back aisle, so I whip out my cell phone and call him. "Hi!" he answers, as though this was going to be a welcoming call.

"Where are you," I ask flatly, running the cart back up the aisle, back in and around all the people I had just passed, moments ago.

"I'm down by the soda. Do we need soda?"

"*No.* We don't need *soda* and the *vitamins* are clear over on the other side of the store."

"Are you sure we don't need soda?"

"We don't need soda! Stay right there, I'm almost out of this aisle."

"Okay. I'm going to pick up some soda."

"We don't need it! Hello? Hello?? *Hello???*"

"I'm here, sorry. Had to put the phone down for a second, I was loading some cases of soda. Why were you yelling?"

"Are you *trying* to upset me or what? Why are you loading soda when I distinctly said, *we don't need soda*?"

"It's only a couple of cases, honey. We can always use soda."

I tersely tell him that I'll be right there and snap the cell phone shut, then jam it into the front pocket of my jeans. I finally maneuver around some tiresomely slow people and their overladen shopping carts, then roll by giant, jolly, inflatable Christmas yard displays and reach the soda aisle.

He isn't there. He isn't near the juices, he isn't near the bottled spring water or the colorful sports drinks. I wheel the cart around and push it briskly back in the direction from whence I came. Maybe he knew the direction that I was coming from, and started back that way in order to meet me, and I just missed him.

He's nowhere. My insides tighten up more. I can just imagine my pancreas and maybe my liver, too, all strictured and blue from the stress of chasing down one wandering Husband in the Sam's Club.

I start pushing the cart through the aisles in the middle, where there are large quantities of jackets, sweatshirts and jeans all piled high on big, square tables. Maybe if I am roughly in the middle of the store, I can spot him more easily. One big, 6'3" guy with a cartful of soda that we don't need, how hard can it be to find him?

Pretty darned hard if you're in the sweatshirts and you suddenly catch a glimpse of his head waaay down there where the miles of freezer cases are located.

Oh, *no*, you think, swiveling that cart around as fast as you can. Huge freezer cases that are full of things like frozen lime tequila flavored chicken wings, and those gigundo tubs of German potato salad that he swears he'll eat and never does… but meantime it takes up all the shelf space in your fridge, wedged tightly against the handy 24-packs of yogurt that he'll be sure to pick up. No, no, and no. It can't be allowed. I stab his number into my cell phone again.

"Hi, honey!"

I'm going to punch him as soon as I get to that frozen food aisle, so help me.

"*Where* are you? I'm getting really *upset*, I've been chasing you through half the store!"

"Why are you getting so excited? We're in the same store. I thought you might stop to look at all the nice Christmas decorations they had on display, so I came over here."

"Where is here?"

"Over here near the potato salad. They have tapioca pudding, too."

"Don't you dare put potato salad in that cart! Or a 5 pound tub of tapioca pudding!"

"It's only a twin pack of 3 pound tubs, honey. What would I do with 5 pounds of tapioca pudding?"

"I am not even going to tell you what I want to do with the damned pudding. Stay there. Stay *there*. I'm coming over to pudding, just *stay* there."

I can't get to the pudding place as fast as I want to, because Sam's has all these little food serving stands set up near the frozen food cases. An elderly woman wearing a fake chef's hat is handing out samples of barbecue somethings on toothpicks and this is creating quite a traffic jam. I am forced to go past where I wanted to turn, go down to breads instead, and then wheel around to come up by the pudding place.

Where he is supposed to be standing, not putting potato salad into his cart, but he isn't standing there. Or anywhere.

Along with my strictured pancreas and liver, my jaw starts to ache from grinding my teeth together. I don't care now about banging into other people's carts, they should be getting out of my way...if they don't recognize a highly stressed woman with a strictured liver trying to get past them, its their own damned fault.

I viciously jab at the little plastic numerals on the cell phone, muttering loudly enough so that several people give me nervous sideways glances as I stomp by them.

"Honey, why do you keep calling me? I thought you were coming over to the pudding?"

"You're not *in the pudding. I* was just there, you *weren't.*"

"Not anymore, no. You didn't come so I went looking for you. I thought maybe you'd be down by candy or something."

"Why on earth would I be down by *candy*, when I told you that I was headed for *pudding*??!!"

"You don't have to yell."

"You're just… you're… just stay there. Stay on the phone and *stay there.* Tell me what aisle number you're on and don't you *dare* hang up this phone."

"Oh, let's see, I'm passing by… uh…4."

"Passing by… don't pass by anything! Just stand there, don't move, are you *listening* to me? *Don't move!*"

"You're going to give yourself a headache, you know. The vitamins are over here. I am simply walking towards the vitamins. Do you want me to pick up some for you?"

I ignore him, hold the phone to my ear with one hand and shove the cart along with the other. As I go past the videos, suddenly I see him. I see him, I see him… hey… stop… I shake the phone and repeat, *stop,* but he keeps walking, looking around. Stop walking! *Stop walking!*

My mind completely blows its gaskets and my vocal cords shift into overdrive. I yell, quite loudly, *"I'VE BEEN CHASING YOU ALL OVER THIS GODDAMNED STORE! STOP WALKINGGG!!!"*

Anyone within a 30 foot radius stopped what they were doing to turn and stare at me. Eyebrows were raised, concerned glances were exchanged. Good *heavens,* the looks on their faces plainly read. Did you hear that woman *scream*? Their heads swiveled around to see who the unfortunate victim was on the receiving end of my vitriol.

I see Husband close his cell phone and snap it back onto the holder hooked to the waistband of his jeans. He walks very calmly back towards me, pushing a cartful of stuff. He stops his cart right next to mine as I stand there, glowering at him. I'm trying to calm my breathing, and trying harder to convince myself that there are really too many witnesses for a proper homicide. Best to wait until I get him back in the truck, where the windows are deeply tinted.

Out of the corner of my eye, I can see people shaking their heads back and forth in disbelief and sympathy for the poor man associated with such a shrewish, screaming creature… me.

My eyes are narrowed into slits, my hand is curled in a fist around my cell phone. My body has released adrenalin or something, and I am shaking slightly.

Husband glances down into my empty shopping cart and then looks back up at me.

"We really don't have the time for a lot of shopping right now, honey. We have to get to Lowe's."

He turns and walks down the aisle to stand in line at the checkout. I stand there and stare at the back of his head, thinking… I could murder him right now, and no jury on earth would convict me. Would you?

MELTDOWN

There are times when Husband causes me to completely lose my mind. My mind is where Sanity lives, along with a few other Worthies such as Patience, Composure, Forbearance and Intestinal Fortitude (Tolerance and Restraint share a room down the hall).

These are emotional guardians, that protect Husband against the destructive forces I could unleash when he manages to upset me. Which he does nearly every day, unless he is miraculously not busy on a Sunday, and then he manages to upset me no less than, oh, half the damned day. I think it's a quota he tries to fill.

So anyway, there are days when he has overfilled this quota, and the Worthies are quivering from Sheer Idiocy Overload on his part and slam their doors, refusing to come out under any circumstances... even Tolerance and Restraint have thrown in the towel and said, dude, you are on your own.

When this has happened, I am prone to a syndrome known as, Lost My Mind. There are symptoms, with varying levels of intensity, that lead up to the development of this syndrome.

For example: The alarm clock rings on Husband's side of the bed at 6:15 am every morning. It does not wake him up. It wakes *me* up.

I lie there, groggy, waiting for him to turn off the alarm, which he never does, because he is asleep. So I nudge his shoulder and say sleepily, "Hey, turn off the alarm." He reaches over in his sleep and hits the snooze button, but does not switch off the actual alarm button. He resumes snoring.

The alarm goes off again at 6:25 am. It does not wake him up. I am semi-awake and hear it, but I am still very tired. He does not turn it off, so I push against his shoulder and say,

"Turn *off* the *alarm.*" He reaches over in his sleep and hits the snooze button and snores. (Level One = initial irritation + benign contact)

The alarm goes off at 6:35 am. It does not wake him up. I am now awake but still pretty tired. He does not turn it off, so I *push* him *harder* on the shoulder and say, *"Turn off the damned alarm!"* He reaches over in his sleep and hits the snooze button. Snores. (Level Two = irritation + mild profanity + purposeful physical contact)

The alarm goes off at 6:45 am. It does not wake him up. I am awake, tired, and *punch* him on the shoulder saying, *"Goddammit, what's WRONG with you? Turn OFF the ALARM!"*

He reaches over in his sleep... hits the snooze button... snores. (Level Three = irritation + profanity + intentional physical contact)

The alarm goes off at 6:55 am. It does not wake him up. I wait a few seconds, hands pressed over my ears. He doesn't turn it off. I uncover my ears and *lunge* my body to the left, trying to climb over him so I can smack the snooze button and find the damn switch to turn off the alarm myself.

He pushes me off with one hand, mumbles, turns on his side and hits the snooze button with the other hand... and snores. I flop back down and pull a pillow over my face, crossing my arms over it. (Attempted physical intervention. Level Four developing, despite the absence of verbal profanity)

The alarm goes off at 7:05 am. It does not wake him up. I rip the pillow off my face and whack him over the head with it, yelling, *"TURN OFF THE GODDAMNED ALARM!!!"*

I whack him a few more times with the pillow for emphasis as he finally hits the snooze button... *gurglesnortlecough... snooore...* (Level Four = extreme irritation + enhanced profanity + deliberate, decisive physical encounter)

The alarm goes off at 7:15 am. It does not wake him up. I lie there, hands over my face, making angry, anguished noises like,

AAARRGGHH!!!" Lie there and listen to the incessant *BEEP! BEEP! BEEP! BEEP! BEEP!* Turn on my right side and *kick* both my feet backwards, like a mule, into his legs. With each word that I yell, I kick him. *"TURN (kick) OFF (kick) THE (kick) FUCKING (kick) ALARRRMMMM!!! (KICK)"*

He stirs, mumbles, "whadyouhitmefor" and shifts his body closer to the far edge of the bed, pulling most of the covers over with him, finally hits the snooze button and...snores. (Level Five = anger + explicit profanity + forceful physical impact, indicating imminent loss of mind)

The alarm goes off at 7:25 am. It does not wake him up. I throw myself out of bed and stomp over to his dresser, where he always keeps a bunch of tools on top. I peer intently into the semidarkness, trying to find a hammer. Can't find one. But a pair of his size 16 sneakers are on the floor, next to the dresser.

Having Lost My Mind, I pick up a huge sneaker, hold it firmly and *WHAPWHAM!* it several times on top of the hapless alarm clock. It stops its incessant bleating and falls over on its side, defeated and hopefully silenced forever more.

This is what can occur when I have Lost My Mind.

Hey, it could've been a lot worse.

I mean, I could've hit Husband over the head with that size 16 sneaker. Or found that hammer, after all...

HARD KNOCKS

Husband has always been drawn to anything that has an Asian flair or influence to it. Doesn't matter what it is, if an object is remotely Asian, he likes it and wants it in his possession. He collects it all: tea sets, saki cups, foo dogs, silk scarves, fans, Buddhas, geisha dolls, samurai swords, martial arts films, gongs, pagodas, jade, carved temple thingies, those little enameled balls that chime when you shake them, and anything with Asian calligraphy... even if it's just on a set of paper wrapped chopsticks originating from the Hong Kong Palace All You Can Eat Buffet.

He has cabinets full of this stuff, and what doesn't fit in the cabinets are in packing boxes stored in his closet and in everyone else's closet.

(Side Note: he's never been out of the USA in his life to any Asian country. Closest he has ever gotten is the China Pavilion and Japan section at Disney World in Orlando. I could *not* get him out of those Ginza style stores.)

So anyway, this endless fascination and obsession with all things Asian meant that it was only a matter of time before he decided to take martial arts. This was made easier by the fact that a guy in our neighborhood was very big into this sort of thing, in fact, he was sort of famous. I won't name names, but he was one of those titles like, Grand Master-San of the Universe of Break and Bust Things Up, or something like that. Oh, and he was a black belt, Husband informed me, which is the highest rank of colored belt you can achieve.

I always thought a black belt was just that, a black belt... *nooo*, there are degrees of black. This guy was like, at some Upper Echelon of belt blackness. Now, I hadn't known this guy was into karate when we first met, so when I found out that he owned a martial arts school, I said, "Ohhh, martial arts, like, um, Taekwondo or something, right?"

He lifted his eyebrows and informed me that Taekwondo was strictly for pussies and fags. I hadn't realized that political in-fighting, name calling and prejudicial attitudes extended into the martial arts, *sorry.*

Grand Master-San owned a *KARATE* school and Husband decided to join.

Classes were held three times a week and this caused an argument, initially, between Husband and me, before it escalated into an all-out war. Husband was a workaholic and rarely made it home for birthdays, school events, holidays, vacations, injuries, illnesses or catastrophes of any sort. How he was going to find the time for a karate class, was a mystery for me…until he started to rearrange his *entire* schedule and make time for the class, before he ran back to finish work in the evening.

This did not sit well with me *at all,* because if he could make the time to get sweaty, make weird fighting noises and try to break things, surely he could make it home for dinner once a month, or attend one of the kids school events.

One night of practice led to two nights of practice, and two nights led to three nights a week, as I waged a losing war against the lure of the Orient. The sight of his white *karategi* (gi or ge, if you prefer) was guaranteed to make my blood pressure and Irish temper rise to unhealthy levels.

So, to make my point how selfish it was for him to choose karate class over, say, listening to his daughter sing off-key in a school recital, I began to do the usual petty things for revenge. I involved the older children in this conspiracy, of course. If the phone rang and we had answered Hello, and then discovered that it was a karate class person who wanted to leave a message or speak to Dad, the kids or I would then say loudly, *"Wongs*

Wings!" And then speak in nothing but unintelligible pidgin Asian/English until the person became frustrated and hung up.

Keith was the most talented in this area. Lori was the worst and gave up trying, handing the phone off to me or one of her brothers. She was torn, poor Lori. On the one hand, she was upset that her father rarely had time to do things with her or her brothers, and went to this karate class instead…but on the other hand, she was tender-hearted and felt that we were all picking on Daddy. Which we were.

How could I *not* pick on Daddy? How often did I get the chance for even the *slightest* sort of Karmic payback for all the moments in our marriage that he had caused me to become completely and utterly insane? We all told her to get over it and kept chattering in false tongues when the karate people called.

Another tactic was an age old one; I simply lost his karate uniform accidentally on purpose. I'd stash it in places where it wasn't like, *obvious* that I had attempted to hide it. He kept it in a gym bag, and sometimes I would remove it from the gym bag and put it under all his jeans in the bottom drawer or something… just to make it look as though he had *perhaps* done this himself, and forgotten. It made him search, and since he is 6'3, bottom drawers are harder for him to reach. Which is why I did it.

After every practice, he would toss the sweaty uniform down the laundry chute, and usually, I'd wash it, fold it, and put it back on the bed… usually. Sometimes I would wash everything *except* the uniform and let it sit there… damp with sweat in the beginning, but stiff and smelly and all crinkled up in two or three days.

He would run home from work just before class, discover it missing, rush around trying to find it, search the drawers, and ask everyone if they had seen it.

The kids would just shrug and say, "Why, no, Daddy, we surely didn't see that karate uniform. Mommy, have you seen dear Daddy's uniform?"

Mommy would have a careworn look on her face, be leaning against the stove, trying to just make a hot cup of tea after a long, hard day. She'd sigh and rub her forehead tiredly to clear her thoughts, and say in an exhausted tone of voice, "Oh, let me think, um… it's not in your bag? You checked the drawers, right? Because last week you left it in a drawer… are you sure that you put it down the chute to be washed? ~sigh~ I guess I can walk all the way down the basement stairs and check for you."

By this time, Husband has dashed downstairs and then dashed back up, with the smelly, balled up mass of sweat-hardened heavy cotton clutched in his hand. "Look!" he'd cry, whacking it against the side of the counter, trying to get the jacket to crack loose from the pants, "You didn't wash my uniform!"

He'd thump, pull and beat on it with his hands while I looked mostly guilty and saddish about this turn of events.

I'd say, "Sorry, but I was so tired and the children did this and the dog ate that and the car wouldn't…" He would re-appear in the middle of my Litany of Woe, gym bag in his hand, stuffed with the crusty uniform and out the door he'd go. I never once felt bad.

He started getting hurt in karate class. His was a white uniform tied with a white belt, which signified that he was a beginner, a novice. From where I was standing, this just meant that the other belt colors felt free to beat up on him more, under the guise of "helping him advance."

I came to consider this a good thing. He deserved some pain for ignoring the children and me. He got bruised, he got battered. He got battered bruises. I would see them on his body late at night after he took a shower, as he patted himself dry, wincing. I'd glance at him and say casually, "More bruises, huh? Gee, and those look like they really hurt, too."

"No," he'd answer, now rubbing briskly with the towel to show that he could handle it, once he saw me watching him. "I don't even feel them, really. I'm used to it."

His belts changed color as the classes advanced, as did the bruises and level of injuries. Blue belt to match the ever present body bruising, which was also on the entire surface of his hands, as he began to break boards.

"Great," I'd say, crossing my arms over my chest in anger. "By all means, let's engage in an activity which could conceivably break the bones in your *hands*. You're only a surgeon, you don't need your *hands*. Explain to the patients how you're going to perform delicate surgery on their bodies with your broken *hands*. Maybe you can hold the scalpel in your teeth."

Yellow belt came next, to match the fading yellow bruises which were always next to the new bruises, as he now tried to break *stacks* of boards and other stupid things. Not just with his hands, but with his feet, too. He limped around on the weekends, but I had no sympathy for an idiot who went around trying to kick cement blocks in half, barefoot. ("It was only that one time, honey, to see if I could.")

I told him, "You need to limp right on up this ladder and screw these cabinets to the wall." We were in the process of building a new kitchen, and if he had the time to kick his fellow man three times a week, I reasoned, then surely he could manage a few screws to keep his wife happy.

Green belt was awarded, which was a near match for the shade his face turned when he broke a rib and I found out and gave him a hug. He had gotten kicked in the chest after a mock-fight called, Bull in the Ring. Some guy with a brown belt was the Bull, and Husband ran into a side kick that he hadn't anticipated and the Bull broke one of Husband's ribs.

He came home holding the gym bag protectively across his chest and walking very, very carefully.

"What's wrong," I asked?

"Nothing," he said, but his voice was careful, too… strained, like it was an effort to talk.

"What happened?"

"Nothing," he said, setting the gym bag down carefully and just standing there.

"Are you going to take a shower now?"

"No," he said, just standing there.

"So... want me to help you off with your jacket?" I moved towards him and a look of alarm flitted across his face.

"*NO*. No, I'm fine, I don't need help. Thank you." And he just stood there.

Little demons inside my head were whispering furiously... *Husband-san does not want your touch... Confucius say you must investigate; it is your sacred duty...*

So I took a step forward, wrapped my arms around his waist and *squeeeezed* hard, hugging him, saying, "Ohhh, it's so nice to have you home."

He turned greenish, moaned, and pulled away just in time to make it over to the laundry room sink and throw up.

That's what happens when you break a rib and someone hugs you, you get nauseous from the pain and throw up. It's also what happens when you try to eat a meal after you have a newly broken rib, you get nauseous and throw up. You then can't lie down in bed to sleep after a newly broken rib, you get nauseous and throw up. So for about three days all Husband did was throw up, stand, starve, throw up, stand, attempt to sleep in a chair, throw up, and stand. Hugging him was forbidden. I enjoyed every minute of it.

During a session on judo holds and jujitsu throws, he blocked a kick that swelled his knee up with a baseball sized hematoma, which means a big fat ball of blood and fluid under the skin. Originally, I thought that this injury occurred after he stepped on a kitchen drawer... it's a long story, tell you later... and crashed through the whole thing into the cabinet below, smashing his knee.

But recently, I found out he had totally *lied* at the time, and covered up this injury by blaming it on *me*, who had made him climb on the ladder to put up more cabinets. He knew I would be pissed off about him getting kicked and injured in class again. (I never felt guilty originally, you realize, when he *did* break that drawer and fell through the entire cabinet, because it was clearly his fault for being stupid and not listening to me. Finding out that he got *kicked* in that knee and then *lied* about it, well…that's how this story got started. It's his own damned fault that the entire world now knows the truth.)

He earned a brown belt, which was right under the big one, the black belt! We're almost at the height of our dumb ass accidents! And wife is now considering things like getting one of the kids to sneak out back after Daddy dashes home from work to get ready for that fucking class, and stick a nice sharp spike into Daddy's truck tires.

Oh, get a grip, I didn't do it. Wanted to. Didn't.

During this phase he nearly broke his neck, but settled for separating his right shoulder, instead. See, everyone in the class was playing this really fun defense game called Belt Choke. A student was the *Choker*, and another student was the *Chokee*. The Choker came up behind the Chokee (who pretended they hadn't noticed) and wrapped a leather belt around the Chokee's neck, pulling it tight.

The Chokee then has to do a semi-turn, grab the Choker with a powerful grip, and while leaning slightly forward, *hurl* the evil Choker over their shoulder to crash on the ground, where he supposedly becomes disheartened or disenchanted or something, and decides not to choke you anymore.

The first time around in this exercise, Husband was the Chokee. He got choked and summoned powerful karate powers, and overthrew the perpetrator to the ground below. Victorious! Then, it was his turn to be the Choker.

(Side note: This is a *class*. No one is actually in danger of getting choked to death by a leather belt. Word would get out if that happened and enrollment would drop, that sort of hing. So while learning to defend themselves against possible criminal attack, the students are supposed to understand that all attack and defense moves, *aren't real ones.* You're not supposed to try to *maim* your fellow students while learning a move. Punches are supposed to be pulled back, kicks to the face are not actually supposed to break your opponents teeth, etc.)

So anyway, Husband was now the Choker and walks up behind a male student and chokes him with the leather belt. This overzealous Chokee, who obviously never read my side note, proceeds to grab Husband and hurl him over his shoulder. Now, when Husband previously threw this same guy, he *hung onto him, like he was SUPPOSED to,* so that the guy wouldn't crash hard and get hurt…but this guy doesn't return the favor. He uses all of his strength while tossing and Husband goes sailing through the air, all 6'3 and 300 pounds of him, to land in a thunderous crash on the floor.

He tells me later: "I realized, dang, I'm going to land on my head and probably break my neck. Wife will be mad. So at the last second I twisted, tucked my head in, and decided to land on my shoulder, instead."

Yeah, I was ever so much happier when he simply separated his shoulder and it took weeks to heal, which meant that he couldn't put the rest of the cabinets and lights up in the new kitchen. If he had broken his damned neck, he'd have been helpless on a stretcher, and I could have yelled at him for as long as I wanted to… well, at least until hospital security asked me to leave. Life is so unfair at times.

One night after practice, I heard his truck pull up in the back driveway. He didn't come in to say hi, I'm home, like he usually did, so I assumed he must have gone straight upstairs to get out of that sweaty uniform.

I was in the new family room, which was in back of the new kitchen, and in the process of painting primer on the walls.

One of my younger sons comes up to me and says, "Dad ha
toilet paper sticking out of his nose."

I frown and say, "He has what?"

"He has toilet paper sticking out of his nose. You shoul
come see."

So I lay my roller down in the paint tray and walk through th
new kitchen to the old kitchen, which is now our new laundr
room/storage pantry. It has a new double utility sink, set in
nice new countertop with cabinets underneath. Standing at th
counter is Husband, wearing only his white karate pants. He i
bent over the sink, scrubbing at something.

I'm standing a little behind him and I am barefoot, so h
hasn't heard me walk up. I lean against the doorway in a relaxe
pose, hands in the pockets of my paint overalls. I give a lou
COUGH.

He jumps and turns to face me. In his hands is the whit
jacket of his karate *ge*. It's dripping water all over the floor an
the front of it is covered in blood.

My eyes rest on the jacket... take in the water puddling or
the floor... then I let my gaze trail from his feet *allll* the way
up to his face. Where I see two long, blood-soaked tubes o
white toilet paper, rather like poorly constructed tampons
protruding from the nostrils of what used to be his nose.

I tilt my head and focus on the swollen remains of the nose
which is shoved sideways on his face, and resembles a squashed
banana. Neither one of us is saying a word.

"So... how did class go tonight?" I ask, nonchalantly.

"Fine," he says.

I nod, never taking my eyes off his banana nose. "Anything
happen in class you want to tell me about?"

"No. Why do you ask?"

"Oh, no reason." I could have stood and gloated or chortled
or done any number of things, but instead I just smiled and
went back to finish priming the new family room walls. Some

things are best savored when you only indulge yourself a little at a time, don't you think?

Later that night when we were getting ready for bed, I watched him stand in front of the bathroom mirror and push on his nose, trying to center it, but it hurt way too much and he had to stop.

"Give it up already," I said, "Your nose is *broken*. You need to see a doctor."

"It's not broken. It's just bruised and a little bent. When the swelling goes down, I'll realign it."

"You need it x-rayed," I insisted, "and you need it set properly... maybe even pinned. This is not a set of tires, you can't realign it."

"I can absolutely realign it, I have the skills. I'm a surgeon. I don't need to see a *doctor.*"

"You need to see a nose guy and let *him* fix it. What are you going to do, walk around the rest of your life with that banana shoved under your *eye?*"

"It is *not* under my eye. It's simply a little off center. I will handle this in a few days."

In a few days it was apparent even for him, that a broken nose hurts like hell when you use your fingers and try to mash it back into place. He was forced to go to an ENT specialist (ear, nose, throat) who took an x-ray and cheerfully told him that it was broken and displaced, and really should have a pin put through it in surgery, to hold it in place while it healed.

Which of course, Husband vetoed, saying, "You have the tools right here, just push the bones back, I'll be fine." Nose Doc warns the stubborn ass surgeon that this could be really painful, and the ass waves his front leg... er, hand, and says he can handle it. He takes karate, you know.

Nose Doc says, "Well, you're going to have to hold *really still,*" and of course, Doc Ass says no problem and grips the padded armrests of the treatment chair he is sitting on. He then spies me still standing in the room and tells me, "Honey, really you can go outside and wait. I don't want you to get upset o become faint during this procedure."

"Wild fucking horses could not drag me from this room, I say, smiling sweetly at him and walking right up to the sid of the chair. Nose Doc wisely does not argue with me as h readies two hypodermic needles, each with a satisfyingly long thin needle.

"Oh, are you going to shoot these into his nose?" I ask, "T numb it up?"

Nose Doc says yes and tells Husband to put his head bacl and not move. I was anticipating a series of injections aroun(the injury, like when the kids get stitches, which would hav been fun to see him squirm through. But instead, to my delight Nose Doc shoves the nice, long needle *up* into Husbands nostri and injects…pulls it back, pushes it in, injects and probes an(injects until finally, the syringe is empty. He then repeats thi with the other nostril.

Husband has not moved, but is gripping the armrests s(hard, his knuckles are white. He informs me that he is breathing through the pain, which he learned in karate, you know.

Nose Doc next takes out some shiny little spoon shape(thingies and shoves them up inside each nostril, *squeeeze* them and rotates and *squeeezes* and works them around *waaa*: up inside the nose and shoves here, pushes there…lots o interesting and enjoyable sound effects go along with all of thi: nasal probing and bone setting.

C R I N C H E L C R A C K L E F u c k C R O G G L E M U M P H L E F U C K CRUNGABADUNGAWRACKACRACKA FUCK!!!!!

And the Nose Doc announces, "Hey, I think that look: pretty good," and stands back for a better view, his head tilting this way and that.

Husband sits with his eyes closed, breathing deeply in and out. I peer critically at the former banana nose. "Are you sure it's straight?" I ask.

It's still swollen, but at least its back in the middle of his face and only slightly tilted at the end. "Maybe you should try it again, just to make sure," I say to the Nose Doc.

Husbands eyes pop open and he says, "*It's fine!*"

"I'm only trying to *help.* There's no need to *yell* at me," I say, looking affronted.

Nose Doc takes long strips of sticky white adhesive tape and drapes them across the nose from top to bottom, then layers them from side to side, constructing a supporting framework so that the bone doesn't shift out of place.

It looks like a giant zinc oxide splotch in the middle of Husband's face, which I pronounce as not too bad. "You'll hardly notice it," I say.

Nose Doc says this has to stay in place for at least six weeks, eight is preferable, and not to remove it or bump the nose until the bone starts to set.

Husband is complaining about the adhesive tape by the time we get into the truck and head for home, and by Day Three, is picking at the sides of it. In one week he has peeled it completely off, claiming the tape is itchy, sweaty and uncomfortable, besides, his nose isn't going anywhere.

I tell him that his nose is going to shift out of alignment, if he doesn't put the tape back on.

He reminds me that I never went to medical school, and therefore, am not qualified to be the judge of such things. This smarmy remark makes me want to punch him right in the face, but I figure that somebody will take care of that for me in karate class at some point, so I grudgingly let it go.

Right before the black belt testing event, everyone in his class started intense practice sessions, to prepare themselves. I had pretty much resigned myself to the fact that this was something he was bound and determined to finish, no matter what the cost and suffering, and no matter what I did to sabotage it and make him see the selfishness of his ways. I would figure out another way to make him pay for it all eventually, but for the time being, I didn't bitch as much.

I even agreed to take the kids to see him in the final testing session, so we could watch him be awarded with his black belt. That is, *if* he passed all the tests and won it. He had to face eight guys in eight different types of attack or something and win the bouts, or at least remain standing at the end, or something macho-assed like that.

Black belt testing comes, it goes, he wins all the bouts he is supposed to and gets presented with his new black uniform and official black belt.

Everybody bows and cheers and claps and takes loads of pictures. Several of the Manly Karate Guys celebrate by smashing their forehead against a wooden board, breaking it in half, as it's held securely by another Manly Karate Guy. Some others attempt to split a baseball bat in half by whacking it with their tongue. I'm *kidding,* they used their forearms to whack against the baseball bats, silly... tongues would obviously just slide right off. I was serious about the foreheads smashing into the wooden boards, though.

There was a small celebration afterwards. We ate cake and drank Hawaiian punch and soda and raised our cans in salute as the Manly Karate Guys tried to out-man one another by smashing hard objects against their various body parts. Kids were aping these talented creatures and smashing soda cans against their foreheads, or a nearby friend's forehead.

I stayed near the cake and volunteered to cut slices for everyone, keeping a large, sharp knife in my hand at all times. I checked my watch every three minutes to see when we could go home, before Lori and I reached dangerous levels of testosterone exposure.

I had purchased a graduation gift from Spencer's Gifts in the mall for Husband, and the kids and I all signed our names on the tag. It was a small motorized hamster, dressed in a black *gi*, holding tiny nunchuks in its paws. It had a little black bandanna tied around its furry brow... kind of a rodent-like Mr. Miyagi.

When you squeezed its little paw, it immediately started gyrating back and forth while wildly flailing its arms, causing the miniscule nunchuks to whirl round n' round in circles, while the hamster sang in a squeaky falsetto, *EVERYBODY WAS KUNG-FU FIGHTING! HYAH! HYAH! IT WAS FAST AS LIGHTNING! HYAH! HYAH!*

It was the stupidest thing I had seen in quite a while, which is why I knew Husband would like it. And he did.

Karate class continued to be a thorn in our marital side for a long time, but the fascination wore off a little, and he did eventually cut the class back to once or twice a week, and sometimes every other week. The school changed location, Grand Master-San retired and moved away, and the people who took over the training didn't have the same powers or something, Husband didn't like "the direction the class was taking."

We eventually moved as well, to the Great Midwest, where there were no karate classes, just snow, cornfields and placid Midwesterners. His black *karategi* and all of the colored belts, the chest protector, fighting mitts, padded helmet, practice swords, and the other 73 crucial pieces of karate equipment he had purchased, were all packed and stored away in large cardboard boxes in our basement.

That stupid ass hamster he still keeps on his dresser, even though it has been years since that graduation party, and its fur has gotten pretty dusty. Every now and then I squeeze its little paw as I walk by and mimic its movements, while saying, "*Hyah! Hyah!*"

Just for fun.

SOMETIMES, IT AIN'T ALL MOONLIGHT AND ROSES

I am getting a stomach virus. Woke up feeling icky and got ickier as the day went on. This is a sneaky virus that creeps up on me, hour by hour. I try to carry on with my day and forget about how bad I feel, trying to fool myself into thinking that maybe it's just something I ate. But although the virus allows me to have this delusion temporarily, I know deep inside that the reality will hit me later in the evening.

Around the dinner hour, I'm starting to get a little queasy but not queasy enough to throw up… yet. It's coming, though. Whatever is making me feel this way, is bound to get bored circulating endlessly in my body for hours and want to get out, and let's face it, there are limited paths out of a human body. None are anatomical garden spots, and all are socially inconvenient when they threaten to leak, discharge or eject something. These actions usually involve some sort of fluid because the body is full of fluids and this is commonly where stomach viruses flourish.

They swim around, make millions of cloned viral buddies and at some point, there simply isn't enough room for everybody. It's gotten crowded, they're becoming rowdy and want to raise some cain before it's too late because the plain fact is, they only have 24 to 48 hours to party, then they're history. White cell commandos will arrive to annihilate them. So they plot… they plan… they send out the unmistakable message to my brain, *Soon, You Are Going To Vomit.*

Husband follows after me as I hold my stomach and walk gingerly upstairs to sit on our bed. "Geezus," I tell him, "I feel terrible."

Husband (homosapien eccentricus)

I need to lie down, but cautiously, because if I move too much my stomach produces an unpleasant pitching, roiling feeling... kind of like seasickness, only on land.

Lying down only helps for a short time, though, because the viral squad goons regain their equilibrium and redouble their efforts to escape. I am breathing very carefully now, feeling saggy... then start to swallow. And swallow. The virals have discovered the esophagus, they see the light waaay up there at the top when my mouth opens, as I talk about how bad I feel. They cluster together, whispering, and begin to make the slow, but steady ascent towards my uvula. I say to Husband, "I'm starting to feel nauseous. Really nauseous, like I'm going to throw up or something."

"You're just tired," he says, "Nobody throws up from being tired. If you were really sick, you'd have a fever. You don't have a fever."

"So what if I don't have a fever, I feel nauseous... really... get me a bucket or a pan or something."

"We don't have a bucket up here. I'd have to go look for one in the garage. You are not going to throw up."

"I am... I can feel it... it's right there, right at the base of my throat. God, I hate to throw up, I hate to throw up!"

"Talking about being sick is just going to make you sick, honey. Think about something else."

"There's nothing else to think of... I need a bucket, just go find me a damned bucket. Oh, *no*..."

I lurch off the bed, because the stomach virus has crept past the base of my throat and is poised and ready to erupt, surely in some vile, messy way. I make it to the bathroom and collapse on the floor next to the toilet. Thank God I cleaned this thing yesterday. I open the lid and lay a hand towel on the seat, resting my forehead against it. *Please*, I bargain with the Vomit Gods, *Just make it a big giant one, okay? Please don't make it a lot of little vomits, don't make me go through this more than once, I'll do anything…*

Husband comes in to ask, "Who are you talking to?"

"The Vomit Gods," I mutter, closing my eyes, "Begging for them to be merciful and quick."

And suddenly, that dreaded salty, metallic taste floods the inside of your mouth and you start to gag and heave. You wrap your arms around that porcelain bowl and hang on for dear life as the viral forces churning in your stomach decide to make a mad dash for freedom, once and for all. You throw up so hard, you're sure pieces of your colon might end up in that toilet bowl, along with everything else in your stomach and lower intestinal tract.

Husband has risen to stand behind me and is holding on to my shoulders, because I am throwing up so forcefully, my body has pitched forward and I've smacked the top of my head against the upraised toilet lid. I am gasping and choking and trying to clear my burning throat.

Husband reaches over to flush the toilet and says, "There, do you feel better now?"

Gulping for air, I manage to answer, "Fuck *NO*, I don't feel better."

"Well," he says, running water in the sink, "at least you're done throwing up." He has a cool, damp washcloth in his hand and holds it to my forehead as I kneel there, head hanging and eyes closed, trying to breathe and not think about how sick I still feel. I don't feel done. I feel *awful*.

I feel so awful that I push his hand away and once again become locked in the grip of a merciless wave of sickness, as I throw up, choke and cough… then spit the long string of drool hanging from my mouth into the water. Scrooching closer to the toilet seat, encircling it with my arms, I rest my cheek against the towel, eyes closed… *pleasepleaseplease let that be the end of it…*

Husband flushes everything away and then sits down on the edge of the tub and mops my chin with the washcloth. "You can't have anything left in your stomach to get rid of *now*," he says, "It can only hold so much liquid, you know."

My stomach hears him and perversely decides to access a spare nausea tank, as I grip the toilet seat and throw up some more. Husband frowns and says firmly, "You need to *stop*, you're going to get dehydrated. If you don't stop throwing up, I am taking you to the *emergency room*."

His tone clearly indicates that I am drastically overdoing the whole stomach virus thing.

I am crying now, feeling sick to death, my entire torso is cramping painfully. "Okay," I sob, "Take me... take me to the emergency room... I think I'm dying..."

"You are not dying, it's just a virus. You're done now, you cannot *possibly* have anything left in your stomach. Trust me, I'm a doctor and know these things." I think my gallbladder and possibly my appendix have joined forces with my stomach and contributed their liquid assets, because unbelievably, I throw up *again*.

"That's *it*," Husband says, tossing the washcloth in the tub and flushing the toilet one last time, "I am taking you *in*." I lie curled in a ball on the bathroom floor, holding my stomach, crying and miserable and sick. He places a clean towel into my hand and hauls me up, guides me down the stairs, through the front door and onto the front seat of his truck.

The hospital is a few blocks away and it takes only minutes to pull in front of the brightly lit emergency room entrance. He maneuvers me out of the truck and into the lobby, parks me in a spare wheelchair, then leaves me there and disappears through a door, as the receptionist eyes me up and down.

I realize I must look like hell, my hair sweaty and sticking out at odd angles, dribbles of stomach content on my t-shirt and sweatpants. I'm too sick to even care about my appearance and just schlump in the wheelchair, looking and feeling pitiful.

It's not a busy night, and besides, Husband works here and knows everybody. He reappears with an aide and I am ushered back in seconds to an empty exam room, hustled into a cotton hospital gown and gratefully lie down on a stretcher. I get rest for about 90 seconds, before I sit bolt upright, gagging. I swallow hard and a young nurse hands me a small, pink plastic kidney shaped basin, officially called an emesis basin, which is just a polite term for vomit catcher. It's a suitable size if I were a nauseous Cabbage Patch doll, but there is no way this little pink pan is going to contain what I am about to mass produce.

I grab for the big blue Welcome Basin she has placed on the foot of the stretcher, with useless articles in it like a toothbrush, comb and tiny toiletries. I dump these out and snatch the basin to my mouth. The nurse snatches it away and thrusts the pink kidney back into my hand, "Throw up in *this*," she orders, "The blue bowl is your *wash basin* if you're admitted."

She sets it over on a countertop, deliberately out of my reach.

"Give it *back*, this isn't big enough," I beg, pressing the towel to my lips. She ignores me and fiddles with an automatic blood pressure device; the cuff of which is wrapped too tightly around my upper arm. She looks about 25 or so, pretty, with perfect blonde hair and wearing scrub pants that are way too tight. I decide I am sick enough to justify hating her. Just for tonight.

I try, I really do *try* to throw up a little less forcefully this time, considering this small container is not a nice big wide toilet bowl, but alas, it's not meant to be. Seemingly every organ in my body contracts in one orchestrated effort, and I clutch the little kidney tightly in my sweaty hands as though it were a life preserver, as the tsunami rises up my throat and spews out of my mouth.

The force of this newest tidal wave hits and effortlessly slops right up over the side of the woefully inadequate little pink basin.

then proceeds to overflow onto my hospital gown, the sheet, and partially onto the tiled floor, where the pretty nurse stares down with a horrified look at her spattered running shoes.

"I *told you* I needed the *blue bowl*," I gasp, coughing the last of it out, long, ropy strands of saliva hanging off of my tongue.

A petite lab tech comes in holding a red carryall of needles and tubes, takes one look, does an abrupt about face and exits. Another pretty young nurse appears, snapping latex gloves on her hands, and she takes away the flooded pink kidney.

I jerk the soiled gown off my shoulders, not caring that the curtains aren't pulled shut or that I am topless and my breasts aren't 25 years old anymore. I throw it on the wet sheet, as the gloved nurse gathers everything in a tightly wadded ball and leaves.

The nurse with the ruined shoes swipes at them with disinfectant towelettes and pushes a button on the wall to summon maintenance. "I'll bring you another emesis basin," she says to me through gritted teeth, as she turns to walk out.

"Just bring me a *toilet*," I call after her, "Just bring me a goddamned *toilet bowl!*"

Husband walks in with a new gown that a passing nurse has stuffed into his hand. I slide my arms into it and he ties the back together for me, as I lean my head against his stomach and repeat that I feel like I'm dying.

"They are going to start you on an IV and some anti-nausea drugs," he says, lowering the head of the stretcher a little and fixing the pillows for me. "And if you have the strength to yell at a nurse, you're not dying anytime soon, honey."

He glances at the floor and says, "What happened?"

"The same thing that's been happening for an hour, I threw up again," I moan, flopping back in my new dry gown. "An evil nurse took the blue bowl away and forced me to vomit on her shoes."

"That's not good," he says.

The doctor comes in and then both men proceed to ignore me as they chat about my vomit, and when it commenced and how many cc's were produced and what the contents appeared to be. I lie there, helpless in my virally diseased state, and wonder what else the contents of vomit could possibly appear to be, *except for vomit*. After years of intense medical training, this is the best they can come up with... God help me...

The petite lab tech reappears and although she looks like a perfectly harmless person, she's obviously best buddies with the spattered nurse. It takes her multiple jabs with nasty, sharp needles ("You'll just feel a little stick," she smilingly lies) until she finally manages to get the IV started. Fluid starts to drip in, to replenish the gallons I have lost. A man shows up with a large mop and a bucket on wheels and swishes the floor clean.

Husband and the doctor stand to one side and continue to yammer away about other people's body parts, various lab results and what the cafeteria still might have to eat at this hour of the night. "Pizza and normal saline, with some potassium in it, absolutely," says Husband, retrieving the big welcome basin from the counter and settling it in the crook of my arm.

"I can't eat *pizza* when I'm possibly *dying*," I pout, curling an arm protectively around my blue bowl, holding it securely against my chest as the doctor walks out of the room.

"The pizza is for me," he says. "You are getting potassium in a saline drip, with some added Zofran to stop the nausea. It might make you a little drowsy." Another teen model type nurse is hooking up two baby IV bags to the big momma IV bag and they all begin to drip slowly into my vein.

Husband stands next to me as I lie there. He glances once in a while at the monitors over my head, which hiss and beep out my blood pressure and heart rate every five minutes. I still feel sick, but am also becoming very tired and my eyes begin to close. "Go to sleep," Husband says. "That's a six hour bag hanging, so go to sleep."

"I don't want to *sleep*," I say peevishly, "If I go to *sleep*, that nurse could sneak in and steal my bowl... she'll want me to suffer, I know it."

"You're being silly, honey. Why would she want you to suffer?"

"For throwing up on her sneakers, Einstein," I answer. I yawn and nestle into my pillows a bit more, resting my chin on the rim of the bowl.

From the doorway the doctor asks how things are progressing and Husband answers, "She's feeling a little better, I think. She's cranky, that's a good sign."

I want to say Fuck You, but I am just too tired, and who is he calling cranky, anyway? I let myself drift off...

Six hours later they unhook my empty IV bags, pull the needle out, patch my bleeding arm with a Band-Aid and pronounce me fit to return home. I don't feel like dancing, but at least I don't feel the urge to throw up on anyone anymore. Husband brings the truck around to the sliding glass doors of the exit, as I am rolled ceremoniously to the curb in a wheelchair and assisted onto the front seat.

It is after midnight when we get back to the house. I am plumb worn out from the whole ordeal, swaying and sleepy from the drugs. All I want to do is lie down for the next month or so. I crawl on my hands and knees up the stairs to our bedroom, manage to stand up, all wobbly, and then collapse on the mattress.

Husband helps me out of my clothes and then pulls one of his giant t-shirts over my head. He tucks me all up in soft quilts and I sigh, watching him. "I feel yucky and sticky," I mutter. "If I wasn't so tired and sick, I'd take a shower. I hate going to bed feeling yucky and sticky."

"You were pretty sick," he says, gathering up my discarded clothes. "But if you need to take a shower, that's fine. I'll help you."

"I could fall... I could get dizzy, fall and hit my head an
be knocked unconscious and drown... I could throw up agai
while I'm unconscious and choke to death."

"You can't drown in a shower, honey, and you aren't going t
throw up anymore, you have too much Zofran in you. Don
be so negative."

"I'm not *negative,*" I answer, as tears unexpectedly slide ou
of the corners of my eyes. "I'm *sick*... and I'm *ugly* tonight, an
probably have vomit in my *hair*... no one else had vomit i
their perfect *hair*... I'm so sick and ugly and old I can sit *nake*
in public, and no one even *noticed.*"

Tears run down my cheeks and runny mucous trickles from
my nose. I'm overwhelmed, ill and coming to grips with th
ghastly picture I must have made in the emergency room.
picture my Husband, surrounded all day by these Barbie dol
twitchy assed nurse types, gossiping... *Did Misty tell you abou
that bitchy old hag we had in room five last night? The one tha
threw up on Brittany's new cross trainers?*

Husband tosses my dirty clothes down the laundry chute
shuts the bedroom door and turns off the light on my
nightstand. He undresses and gets into bed, then hands me hi
t-shirt to dry my eyes. I sniffle and shift closer to him, blow my
nose on the t-shirt and hand it back to him.

"Silly woman," he says, dabbing the snotty damp t-shir
under my nose one more time, "You are *not* old, you *were* sicl
and at the end of a shift in that emergency room, all those nurse:
you saw will be covered in worse things than a little vomit. Anc
you were only half naked, and I noticed. I'll always notice. I'l
always love you, and think you are the most beautiful woman
in the world, even when you get a stomach virus and end up
with vomit in your hair."

He is holding me close, even though I haven't taken a showe
or washed my smelly hair. His actions alone that show he

meant what he said to me many years before, and still does, apparently... *in sickness and in health, for better and for worse.*

Husband isn't the most romantical of men, and saying that he'll love me even with a stomach virus and crud in my hair isn't exactly moonlight and roses, but it's what I needed to hear tonight. It ain't Shakespeare, but it'll do just fine.

BOOK JACKET DILEMMA

zeecee: Knock knock

Halliegirl: Did you come up with something?

zeecee: Pressure... all I get is pressure... doesn't anyone care about *me?*

Halliegirl: I care about you. Now, did you come up with something?

zeecee: Well, I thought and thought and thought and thought...

Halliegirl: And?

zeecee: And then I thought some more... and realized I am just not going to be able to do what everyone wants and expects...

Halliegirl: No one is expecting you to write another Gettysburg Address or anything! You've written hundreds of pages for this book, and you're obsessing over a few paragraphs.

zeecee: Not *obsessing*... exactly...

Halliegirl: You obsess 24/7 over certain things, and this book jacket is one of them. Now let me read what you wrote.

zeecee: The author works from a secret location, known only to a few trusted allies and the FBI. When she isn't embarrassing family members with the content of her writing, she stays busy raising genetically altered glow-in-the-dark mice, constructing a rocket ship to Venus and cultivating talking plants grown from irradiated seeds. She resides somewhere on the planet Earth.

Halliegirl: I'm ready with my verdict. Want to hear it?

zeecee: You hate it... I knew it... you hate it... I'm giving up my writing career to become a hermit and live with the pelicans

Halliegirl: I can't explain this, Zee, but in a really strange way this suits you. Except that you're scared of mice and radiation, of course, and you'd get agoraphobic in deep space and have a major panic attack. If you want to get technical about details.

zeecee: Then how can it possibly be me?

Halliegirl: Probably because if you *weren't* afraid of mice, radiation and deep space, they're the sort of things you'd have for a hobby. Weird stuff.

zeecee: I hope you're saying that with luv

Halliegirl: Totally and completely. I'm just a little disappointed that you didn't give me, your trusted sidekick, an honorable mention.

zeecee: Well, what part did you want to be included in? Did you want to be my co-pilot to Venus?

Halliegirl: Do I get to wear a snazzy, sexy spacesuit? Will my ass be fabulous and encased in something tight, so all the men who read about me will drool?

zeecee: I'll include you as my trusty computerized sidekick who gives me sensible advice... you can be a silvery robot with nice tits that revolve in circles or something and shoot poison darts...

Halliegirl: Zee

zeecee: Wait, I know! You can be the alien queen on Venus when I land, with tentacles and awesome power, and we communicate through the talking plants and work to save the universe...

Halliegirl: Zee

zeecee: What?

Halliegirl: Tentacles and poisoned, revolving tits?

zeecee: It was just *an idea...*

Halliegirl: For some reason, you becoming a hermit and living with the pelicans is starting to sound good.

RANDOM THOUGHTS...

looked up the word RANDOM, and this is what was listed: proceeding, made, or occurring without definite aim, reason, or pattern—odd and unpredictable in an amusing way."

I think that totally explains a lot of the stuff I have in my overloaded brain. So here is some random stuff and a few brain dribbles as well...

In spite of the fact I am left-handed, I can't use my left hand to do anything but write or eat. I use right-handed scissors, throw a ball right handed, catch right handed, etc. It's weird and backwards, kind of like me.

I can't go to sleep for the night unless I've checked all the doors twice, to make sure they didn't accidentally unlock themselves after I checked them the last time.

I do not drive much at night, because my night vision sucks. My day vision sucks too, but at least I have eyeglasses, and it's still one heck of a lot better than trying to squint and see at night. You can't see cops in the dark when you are driving and nearly night blind. Sometimes they catch you speeding. It sucks.

I cannot drive a stick shift anything, and have no desire to learn how.

I cannot change a flat tire on a car, but I can call the Triple A folks.

I cannot recall the PIN number to any of my debit cards, but I do know how to swiftly swipe all my credit cards.

I am totally confused as to why all those morning television/talk shows are so popular. Who the *hell* are these carefully coiffed and trendily out-fitted people at this ungodly hour in the morning, and why do I want to hear what they have to say about *anything?*

I can't barbecue anything fit to eat except maybe a hot dog... and then I either burn it, or somehow get it to fall between the grill bars directly onto the flames. Which isn't what I would call successful barbecuing, but hot dogs are a fairly sturdy food, and they wipe off easily. Just don't tell anyone and they'll never know.

I nearly always use a straw to drink through, because I am paranoid I might choke on too much liquid while drinking from a glass, aspirate some into my lungs and then die after turning a gruesome blue/gray color. I carry straws *everywhere.*

I can't whistle, but I can sing... and on tune, thank you.

I can knit, but have never been able to grasp the intricacies of using a crochet hook. My brain simply won't process it. My sister can crochet beautifully, but she cannot knit. So between the two of us, it evens out somehow.

I refuse to do the Chicken Dance at weddings no matter how many other people are squawking and flapping. I mean please... get real.

I cannot do any sort of math beyond the basic add, subtract multiply or divide... and dividing is tough. But I can whip out a calculator and push the buttons very well.

I can't swim very well, and I absolutely cannot float... no matter what I do, I sink. I can, however, sit on the side of a pool and not fall in.

I detest strawberries, but I like strawberry jelly.

I like the taste of watermelon, but detest watermelon flavored anything.

I cannot drive across a bridge without getting some sort of panic attack. Sometimes they're small attacks, sometimes they

re bigger, but whatever the size, I don't do bridges well *at all*.
o if there is a bridge, I stop well before it and make Husband
rive. If I am driving by myself and *forced* to cross a bridge,
 sing songs loudly, so I can nearly fool myself into thinking,
VE'RE NOT REALLY OVER THAT WATER WAY DOWN
'HERE SO I CAN'T DROWN LA LA LA

I can't make decent fried chicken no matter how closely I
ry to follow a recipe. The breading won't stick to the damned
hicken, and if I do manage to get it to *sort* of stick, it falls off
ince its dropped into the hot fat, so then I have pieces of naked
hicken frying.
Which ain't the same thing.

I don't like sleeping under a top sheet. I prefer a blanket or a
quilt next to my skin. Having a top sheet next to my skin just
nakes it feel like a super big, clingy pillowcase is draped all over
ne. It tangles and gets sweaty. I can't sleep if I am tangled and
weaty.

I miss Freddy Mercury. Queen isn't the same without its
nain queen.

When someone knows you are on a diet and they stand there
istening to you talk about it while munching on a handful of
Reese's pieces, they are not your friend.

I bet there wouldn't be any sexual harassment claims if
everyone were spayed or neutered.

I will not pick up a spider, but worms aren't too yucky.

I do not understand the concept of those automated
ap pools. You swim and swim and swim but you never get
anywhere. Same thing goes for those infinity pools, the ones
vhere the water spills over the side, like a bathtub overflowing?

I just don't get it. Personally, I'd never step inside one of those infinity pools. I would be paranoid that I'd fall right over the edge into oblivion and no one would ever find me.

I don't know how to access the answering machine featured on my cell phone, because I can never recall the secret code to unlock it. So if you have called me and I am not answering any of your messages, that's why.

I brake for dogs, cats, and small furry animals, but I go out of my way to run over snakes in the road. Sue me.

Do you think the Pope ever says *fuck*? I guess if he did, it would be in Italian and most of us would never know anyway, right?

PREQUEL TO:
INSPIRATION IN A JUNK DRAWER

Whenever people discover that you write, be it for profit or pleasure, at some point this question is asked, "Where in the world do you get ideas for the things you write about?"

I have never met an actual published writer in the flesh, so I can't answer for how any of them might answer that, so let's ask myself and see what I say:

Self One : So, Self, tell me, where do you come up with the ideas for the stupid things you write?

Self Two: You forgot ridiculous...

Self One: My apologies, for the stupid and ridiculous things that you write?

Self Two: Thank you for that clarification. Why, inspiration can come from almost anywhere. Life experiences, dreams, memories, oh, so many things. (insert a not-too-lengthy, but thought-ridden pause here) Junk drawers.

Self One: I'm sorry, did you just say junk drawers?

Self Two: Yes, it's typed right there as you can see (points upward). Junk drawers. There is an amazing amount of history and untold tales contained in a junk drawer. It's like a messy time capsule of your life; one that isn't buried outside, but accessible right there in the privacy of your own home. Everyone has a junk drawer, somewhere. Many people have several.

Self One: Do you have a junk drawer, Self?

Self Two: Indeed, I do. Junk drawers are unique and should get more recognition for what they are; bits and pieces of your personal life and family history. There are reasons you collect certain types of junk, keep it for years, then pack it up and carry it with you from place to place.

There are reasons you ponder upon your junk, then decide if it is really meaningful junk anymore, and either toss it away or stash it safely back in the drawer. It represents stages of your life, closure in some areas, indecision in others... junk drawers could be a therapist's dream, if they only bothered to make house calls and insist on inspecting their client's drawers.

Self One: Er... well...

Self Two: The junk drawers, mind you.

Self One: (nodding hastily) Of course, I knew that.

Self Two: (smiling serenely) Of course you did, I'm no foo
Now, it is important to note that no matter how much you tr
not to have a junk drawer, the very fact you can't get rid of you
junk means something. My junk has now increased and fil
two drawers. I don't know why. Maybe I am not *meant* to knov
why yet. The point is, don't fight with your junk. It will reve:
why it is there in time.

Self One: You mean that the useless pencil stubs, pieces c
broken toys, old house keys, coins stuck together with supe
glue, are all going to have something insightful to contribute t
my life some day? That seems a bit far-fetched to me.

Self Two: Naturally, you are not at a point where you ca
understand *why* those are the pieces of junk you just can't bear t
part with. The pencil stubs may represent your desire to sit dow
and write a really serious piece of literary work. To throw then
away might mean you have given that up; subconsciously yo
just can't accept that. Thus, the pencil stubs in the junk drawer.

Self One: I don't really have pencil stubs in my junk drawe
I do have the coins super-glued together, though...

Self Two: Do you in fact have useless pencil stubs *somewher*
in your home?

Self One: Yes, but they're not in a drawer.

Self Two: Irrelevant, my good Self, the very fact that yo
keep useless pencil stubs that can't possibly write well is the ke
issue. They do not necessarily have to be in a drawer; it's junk
I rest my case.

Self One: Are you always this... um...

Self Two: Yes

Self One: That's what I thought, now... where were we... oh
yes, the next section, I assume it will be on junk drawers, then

Self Two: It will indeed. Let us proceed.

INSPIRATION IN A JUNK DRAWER

Human beings have been known to collect things, and a lot of these things could safely be classified as junk. I think that some animals collect junk, too, except they don't keep theirs in a drawer, naturally. I'm not sure about fish or insects, but isn't there a crab or some such creature that keeps rocks in its little lair? That would count as a type of collected item, but I doubt the crab itself views it as junk.

Humans are unique in that they are partial to junk. Drawers are very handy places to stash junk because they're common, in nearly every room of your home. Cars and trucks have glove compartments, but when was the last time you actually put gloves in your glove compartment? You don't, of course, you keep them stuffed in your coat pocket or in the side pocket of the car door which is also a place for more junk.

Glove compartments are used to store maps, papers, a skinny flashlight to read the papers or maps, receipts you didn't want anyone else to see, and in Husbands case, the stash of candy bars your wife will lecture you for stashing.

Junk repositories are everywhere, if we would only take the time to look around and recognize them for what they are.

Pocketbooks hold a lot of junk. Wallets hold smaller bits of junk. Kids pockets hold junk that comes out in the washing machine. Mothers collect it out of the filter and return it to the kid so that they can put it back in the pockets in time for the next wash.

Junk resides in makeup bags. That lipstick you haven't applied in two years, but there's half a stick left and you used to like that color... eye shadow in those tiny plastic cases, so worn down there are just rims of color left around the edges, but still, you keep them... nail polish bottles with tops that you will never be able to unscrew again, thanks to the excess polish you scraped off on the sides while using it originally, that has long since dried to the consistency of concrete. The list of possible junk could be two feet long and mention everything in your cosmetic and personal use arsenal. Let's face it, for some women, your entire bathroom could be a junk drawer.

Kitchens collect fantastic amounts of junk, and since there are lots of drawers in kitchens, they hold a greater variety of it too. Partially melted rubber spatulas, corn on the cob holders that have one prong, collections of old, shreddy sponges under the kitchen sink, wobbly stacks of plastic cream cheese/margarine tubs (most with no matching lids), forks with bent tines, at least a hundred of those little "to go" packets of ketchup, mayonnaise, Arby's sauce, etc.

Need I go on?

Kitchens or laundry rooms are common places where most of the Official Junk Drawer(s) have an honored place. Want to know what is in one of mine? Here's a *partial* list:

>> Nails/Screws/Brackets/Bolts/Nuts/Washers
>> Sunglasses with lens missing/Torn off clothing labels
>> Odd buttons/Twist ties/Old coupons and sales receipts
>> Packet of carrot seeds, half empty/Wooden popsicle sticks
>> Silver Monopoly dog and top hat playing pieces
>> Torn off corner of a dollar bill/Flash cards/Playing cards
>> Barbie shoes/Lumps of hardened Play-Doh
>> Xmas light bulb replacements/Pills for the dog
>> Super glue/Partial roll of ancient Lifesavers
>> Batteries that don't work/Pieces of stale gum
>> Switch plate with not enough screws/Appliance booklets
>> Luggage tags with broken chains/One shoelace
>> Small hand tools/Old emory boards/Mangled paper clips
>> Paint sticks/Paint samples/Scraps of used sandpaper

Before you raise an eyebrow or snicker at my junk drawer contents, how about you show me yours, hmm?

I *thought* so.

Bedrooms and clothing closets can hold lots of junk. Most women have a pair of nylon stockings (or several pair) that have at least one leg full of runs. You know you're never going

) wear the snagged up things, but still, for some reason you
on't throw them out.

Men seem to cling to ancient t-shirts with holes and forever
melly/stained armpit areas, or old, shapeless, floppy socks
where any shred of elastic has long since disintegrated. People
ling to sneakers with the soles falling off or pocketbooks with
roken handles; it's *all* clothing and accessory junk.

Animals don't get into junk as intensely, it seems, although
've seen some gather toys, bones, shoes, etc., and stash them
round... but is this instinct on their part, a sort of gathering
ehavior? It can't be greed, or a status thing.

"I have *way* more slobbered on tennis balls than *you* do, Sparky."

I have to conclude perhaps it's territorial, or they like having
broader choice of things to chew on... I don't know.

I do know that junk gathering begins early in a human's
ife. Start off with your basic new human, a baby, for instance.
'arent(s) buy the baby a lot of baby clothes, furniture, and
quipment. Family and friends can shower them with even more
aby articles. An entire 15 by 15 foot room can be filled with
aby oriented things that are for one single 5 to 9 pound baby.

Inevitably the baby outgrows/doesn't use/or destroys nearly
verything that was bought or gifted for its own small self.
'arents can choose to sell it, re-gift it to someone else's baby,
r... save it.

This might be what begins the whole process of junk
gathering for a new generation. It makes me ask this question:
lo we start saving stuff for our children because our parents
lid it for us? Did we see others doing it for their children and
copy their behavior? Or is it just in our DNA to stash, hide
ind gather things?

Is it a throwback to our prehistoric ancestors that did in fact,
tash, hide and gather things because it meant survival? Or are
he roots of the junk drawer to be found in the era of the Great

Depression, where food, money and necessities were so scarce you hung on to all you could find?

It makes me wonder if medieval people had junk drawers. Well... junk chests? Junk satchels? What would they have kept junk in, and what junk would they have kept? They didn't have super glue or margarine tubs. Maybe they didn't call the things they saved, "junk".

I read somewhere that anthropology types (or is it archeology types) study trash heaps from ancient civilizations... broken pottery, old weapons, things like that. They put together whole scenarios of what people's lives might have been like thousands of years ago, just from the things these people threw away.

I say look at the stuff people *keep*, there's your real insight into what made that person tick. Examine what they held onto or carried about for years. Ask to see the contents of a friend's junk drawer and listen as they babble on about why those bottle caps are in there, or they kept sets of keys to houses they don't live in anymore. You might just be surprised what you discover in those seemingly useless little discards that we all can't seem to let go of.

Just don't touch my twist ties.

THE END...

Ah, the inevitable end. But it isn't, not really...

This was only a small offering of the many bits of flotsam and jetsam taking up space in my head, but there's still plenty of stuff left in there to tell you about, if you want to read about it someday.

I think the next offering from me will be in a somewhat different vein, though. Kid related stories are being constructed, there are a lot of random thoughts on many subjects, some observations on life are being jotted down, and issues are surfacing that need investigating, like growing older and losing people you love.

If these little tales have caused you to smile or laugh, I am glad, however, the next insights into my life may not always be as easy or humorous to read...but they will be, like everything else in this book, real reflections, real reactions and the real me. Thanks for reading... ☺

Z.C.

zcchristie@yahoo.com